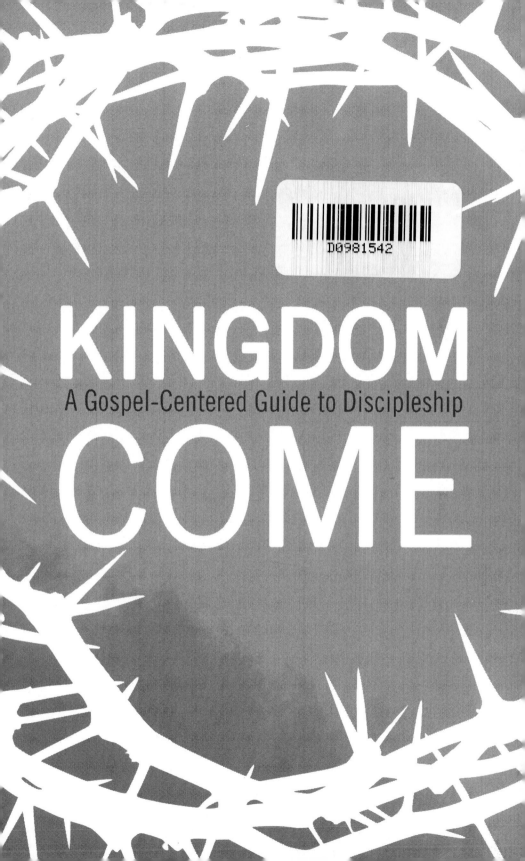

KINGDOM

A Gospel-Centered Guide to Discipleship

COME

TABLE OF CONTENTS

PART 4: PRAYER & COMMUNITY

PART 5: GROWTH & POWER

PART 6: COMMAND & COMMISSION

PART 7: DISCIPLINES & DISCERNMENT

LEADERS GUIDE

INTRODUCTION

WELCOME TO THE JOURNEY

On behalf of those who have been praying for you, the people who have loved you, and the person who first shared Jesus with you, we would like to welcome you to the journey of discipleship. The greatest decision you could ever make is starting a relationship with God. The second greatest decision you could ever make is investing time, energy, and resources toward growing in that relationship with God.

While we understand you may have plenty of questions and thoughts, it is our hope and prayer that over the next several weeks, your life will be radically impacted. What you will find in the pages of this book are seven important foundational chapters dedicated to helping you embrace and understand the Kingdom of God in your life. Also included is a glossary of helpful Biblical terms and a listing of resources for further studies.

Before you get started, we would like to share with you three important decisions worth making as you begin this journey.

FIRST DECISION: TELL SOMEONE

Tell someone about your decision to be discipled and ask them to be in prayer for you over the next seven weeks. Letting other people know will not only help you follow through on your commitment, but will also increase your level of spiritual support.

SECOND DECISION: BE READY AND BE ON TIME

Make sure to fully complete your weekly reading, reflections, and assignments before meeting with your discipler. It's crucial to show up on time and be prepared to discuss what you have learned from the previous week. When you make this decision, it allows you to get the most out of your time being discipled.

THIRD DECISION: PRAY DAILY

Start every morning for the next seven weeks in prayer. We will discuss more about prayer in the weeks to come. Let the first words from your mouth each morning be a portion of the prayer Jesus taught His disciples to pray in Matthew 6: "Father, may your Kingdom come in me and through me today."

Enjoy the rich journey of discovering what it means to be a disciple in the Kingdom of God. May you glorify God with each turning page, find joy in the King and spend the rest of your life seeing His Kingdom come in you and through you.

For more information about Kingdom Come Discipleship visit www.kingdomcomediscipleship.com.

MAKE A
COMMITMENT

Welcome to the exciting journey of becoming a passionate follower of Jesus who has a commitment to living in and extending God's Kingdom. We designed this guide to help you understand the Kingdom of God and what it means to be a disciple of Jesus. Your discipleship leader is prepared and equipped to walk with you.

As you embark on this journey we ask that you fully agree to the following commitment.

ATTEND ALL MEETINGS

I will attend all meetings with my discipler unless hindered by emergencies or serious conflicts.

BE ON TIME EVERY TIME

I will be on time for meetings, so that we can start on time and end on time.

COMPLETE ALL READING AND ASSIGNMENTS

I will complete each chapter and any given assignments before attending discipleship meetings.

FULLY ENGAGE

I will fully engage in discussions, bring questions and share with transparency.

ENCOURAGE AND RESPECT

I will encourage, affirm and respect my discipler.

I _____ make the commitment today on

_____ to fully give myself to this discipleship relationship.

All meetings are private and personal and everything shared will remain private.

PART 1:
THE KINGDOM STORY
THE KING & HIS KINGDOM

PART 1:
THE KINGDOM
STORY

Many people were raised in church settings, reading one inspirational book after another and following Jesus for years without ever knowing the main story of the Bible and the central message of Jesus. The main story of the Bible is a divine love story about the Kingdom of God for the glory of God. The central message of Jesus is a message about this Kingdom.

What is the Kingdom of God? The Kingdom of God is the rule and reign of God and the power and presence of God. It is made available and accessible to us in and through Jesus.

Understanding the story of the Kingdom of God is an extremely important part of being a disciple. What is a disciple? A disciple of Jesus is someone who has a relationship with Jesus and is a follower of Jesus. The term disciple means learner or follower. The primary goal of the Christian life is learning from Jesus and following Jesus. It is knowing Jesus and making Him known.

As devoted followers of Jesus few things are more encouraging, inspiring, and helpful than learning about the story of the

Kingdom of God. When we understand the story of the Kingdom of God our perspective of the Christian life changes. We realize God is about His glory, our joy, and His Kingdom. Let's take a journey through the Bible and unpack this amazing divine love story of the Kingdom of God.

What is the Kingdom of God?

_____

_____

What is a disciple?

_____

_____

THE KINGDOM OF GOD IN THE GARDEN

Genesis, the first book of the Bible, tells the story of God's initial Kingdom on earth. In the first chapter, we learn that God created the heavens, earth, and everything in them. Then, He created the first man and first woman. He placed them in the Garden of Eden and gave them only one restriction. They could eat from any tree in the garden, but they could not eat from the tree known as the "tree of knowledge of good and evil." God ruled and reigned in their life and it was the first place we saw the Kingdom of God on earth.

> *"So God created mankind in his own image, in the image of God he created them; male and female he created them. God blessed them and said to them, "Be fruitful and increase in number; fill the earth and subdue it. Rule over the fish in the sea and the birds in the sky and over every living creature that moves on the ground."*
> **Genesis 1:27-28**

It was not long before Adam and Eve chose not to allow God

to rule and reign in their life. Instead of listening and obeying God, they ate from the one tree they were prohibited to eat from in the garden.

The moment they made this decision, sin entered the world and hijacked the rule and reign of God in their lives. Sin is anything that separates us from God and removes His rule and reign in our lives. Sin always destroys, always divides, and always leads to death.

"When the woman saw that the fruit of the tree was good for food and pleasing to the eye, and also desirable for gaining wisdom, she took some and ate it. She also gave some to her husband, who was with her, and he ate it. Then the eyes of both of them were opened, and they realized they were naked; so they sewed fig leaves together and made coverings for themselves. Then the man and his wife heard the sound of the LORD God as he was walking in the garden in the cool of the day, and they hid from the LORD God among the trees of the garden. But the LORD God called to the man, "Where are you?" He answered, "I heard you in the garden, and I was afraid because I was naked; so I hid." And he said, "Who told you that you were naked? Have you eaten from the tree that I commanded you not to eat from?"

The main story of the Bible is a divine love story about the Kingdom of God for the glory of God.

Genesis 3: 6-11

From that point forward, the Bible tells us that every person ever born, is born into a world of sin and is inherently and ultimately separated from God.

"Therefore, just as sin entered the world through one man, and death through sin, and in this way death came to all people, because all sinned"

Romans 5:12

THE KINGDOM OF GOD IN THE PROMISE

Then God made a promise to a man named Abraham in Genesis 12. It was a promise that God's Kingdom, His rule and reign, power and presence, would come through a group of people at a future time. This group of people would come to be known in scripture as the nation of Israel.

"The LORD had said to Abram, "Go from your country, your people and your father's household to the land I will show you. "I will make you into a great nation, and I will bless you; I will make your name great, and you will be a blessing. I will bless those who bless you, and whoever curses you I will curse; and all peoples on earth will be blessed through you."

Genesis 12: 1-3

THE KINGDOM OF GOD IN THE TENT

God promised Abraham the future Kingdom on earth would be through his family tree. Yet not long after this promise was given, Abraham's descendants decided to pursue their own desires and to no longer live under the rule and reign of God. They were eventually brought into slavery under the nation of Egypt. For over 400 years they waited for God to rescue them. God not only rescued His people, but also did so through an unlikely leader named Moses.

In the book of Exodus, we learn about God delivering His people from slavery in a miraculous way and setting them up to enter a new land. They would not enter this new land, known as the Promised Land overnight. Instead, as a result of their lack of faith, they would find themselves wandering the desert for forty years. It was in the desert that God's rule and reign was made available to them through the tent of meetings.

The tent of meetings, also known as the tabernacle, was the place God's presence dwelled among the people. It was the place that they came to make sacrifices to God for their sin. A sacrifice was always needed for the people to have a restored relationship with God.

> "Now Moses used to take a tent and pitch it outside the camp some distance away, calling it the "tent of meeting." Anyone inquiring of the LORD would go to the tent of meeting outside the camp."
>
> **Exodus 33:7**

THE KINGDOM OF GOD IN THE TEMPLE

After forty years, the people entered into the Promised Land and started to settle and build. After many years had passed, they began to take notice of other nations and started to desire a human king to rule and reign over them. God heard their cry and decided to give them what they wanted. The people of Israel appointed a man named Saul as their first king.

> "So all the elders of Israel gathered together and came to Samuel at Ramah. They said to him, "You are old, and your sons do not follow your ways; now appoint a king to lead us, such as all the other nations have." But when they said, "Give us a king to lead us," this displeased Samuel; so he prayed to the LORD. And the LORD told him: "Listen to all that the people are saying to you; it is not you they have rejected, but they have rejected me as their king."
>
> **1 Samuel 8:4-7**

The prophet Samuel anointed Saul as Israel's first king. They would later come to regret this decision, because of his unstable leadership. After forty years, God decided to rescue the people once again by anointing a new king. This king would lead the people in an entirely new direction and would become one of the most beloved people in scripture. The new king that was anointed by God to lead the people was a man named David.

David noticed that God's presence was dwelling in a tent, while he himself slept in a palace. One of the things that David did while he was king is ask God if he could build Him a temple. God did not allow David to build the temple, but He did give permission to David's son Solomon. It is under Solomon, the third king of Israel that the temple is built.

"After the king was settled in his palace and the LORD had given him rest from all his enemies around him, he said to Nathan the prophet, "Here I am, living in a house of cedar, while the ark of God remains in a tent." Nathan replied to the king, "Whatever you have in mind, go ahead and do it, for the LORD is with you." But that night the word of the LORD came to Nathan, saying: "Go and tell my servant David, 'This is what the LORD says: Are you the one to build me a house to dwell in? I have not dwelt in a house from the day I brought the Israelites up out of Egypt to this day. I have been moving from place to place with a tent as my dwelling. Wherever I have moved with all the Israelites, did I ever say to any of their rulers whom I commanded to shepherd my people Israel, "Why have you not built me a house of cedar?"'

"Now then, tell my servant David, 'This is what the LORD Almighty says: I took you from the pasture, from tending the flock, and appointed you ruler over my people Israel. I have been with you wherever you have gone, and I have cut off all your enemies from before you. Now I will make your name great, like the names of the greatest men on earth. And I will provide a place for my people Israel and will plant them so that they can have a home of their own and no longer be disturbed. Wicked people will not oppress them anymore, as they did at the beginning and have done ever since the time I appointed leaders over my people Israel. I will also give you rest from all your enemies. "'The LORD declares to you that the LORD himself will establish a house for you: When your days are over and you rest with your ancestors, I will raise up your offspring to succeed you, your own flesh and blood, and I will establish his kingdom. He is the one who will build a house for my Name, and I will establish the throne of his kingdom forever."

2 Samuel 7:1-13

God's rule, reign, power, and presence moved from a tent into a temple. The temple became known as the place where God's presence dwelt. It was there that people would come to receive forgiveness for sin and a restored relationship with the living God by offering sacrifices.

THE KINGDOM OF GOD IN THE VISION AND THROUGH THE PROPHETS

Years after Solomon, the Israelites once again made the decision to move away from the rule and reign of God and pursue their own desires and their own kingdoms. This decision to turn away from God led them back into slavery and into the rule of foreign countries. In the midst of this crisis, God sent one prophet after another giving the people hope and a future vision of the day when God would once again rule and reign over them.

> *"In my vision at night I looked, and there before me was one like a son of man, coming with the clouds of heaven. He approached the Ancient of Days and was led into his presence. He was given authority, glory, and sovereign power; all nations and peoples of every language worshiped him. His dominion is an everlasting dominion that will not pass away, and his kingdom is one that will never be destroyed."*
>
> **Daniel 7:13-14**

> *"For to us a child is born, to us a son is given, and the government will be on his shoulders. And he will be called Wonderful Counselor, Mighty God, Everlasting Father, Prince of Peace. Of the greatness of his government and peace there will be no end. He will reign on David's throne and over his kingdom, establishing and upholding it with justice and righteousness from that time on and forever. The zeal of the LORD Almighty will accomplish this."*
>
> **Isaiah 9:6-7**

Throughout this period of history, one prophet after another came prophesying about a future day when God would send His Messiah to rule and reign and to establish His Kingdom forever.

The word messiah means anointed one. It is a term that describes one who deliverers, rescues, and saves. This was the expectation and hope for the future when one day God would once again rule and reign in their lives.

As the Old Testament ends, 400 years of silence begins. In that time there is no record of a prophet speaking or a new book being written, just silence.

THE KING OF THE KINGDOM OF GOD

With the beginning of the New Testament, the silence is broken. The great and glorious Father sends His Son, Jesus to the earth. And when Jesus comes, He comes to bring God's Kingdom. He comes as the King of the Kingdom.

The name Jesus in the Hebrew language means God saves. Christ is not the last name of Jesus, but rather a title given to Jesus. Christ is the Greek translation for the Hebrew word Messiah. As we mentioned earlier, the word Messiah means anointed one. It is used in the Bible when talking about a king. The name Jesus Christ means Savior King.

The most frequent title given to Jesus in the four gospels of the New Testament is Son of Man. This is a direct fulfillment of the vision given in the book of Daniel. The central message of Jesus is the message of the Kingdom of God.

What does the name Jesus Christ mean?

_____

_____

"After John was put in prison, Jesus went into Galilee, proclaiming the good news of God. "The time has come," he said. "The kingdom of God has come near. Repent and believe the good news!"

Mark 1:14-15

The rule and reign of God seen in the garden, then in the tent , then in the temple, is now made available and accessible through the great King of Kings, Jesus. Jesus comes as the King to forgive sin, restore a broken relationship with the Father and bring the rule and reign of God to earth. This is the great and wonderful divine love story.

"For God so loved the world that he gave his one and only Son, that whoever believes in him shall not perish but have eternal life."

John 3:16

> **The gospel is the good news of Jesus and His Kingdom. The gospel exposes our sin, but it also exposes our worth.**

Now for people to receive forgiveness and restoration from their sin they no longer need to go to a tent, or a temple, or to a priest with a sacrifice. Instead they can go directly to Jesus. He lived, taught, died, and rose from the dead victoriously to bring the Kingdom of God on earth.

This is the gospel. The word gospel means good news. The good news according to scripture is that Jesus the King of Kings has come to bring the Kingdom of God. It is through His life, death, and resurrection that every person is invited into a relationship with God. The gospel exposes our sin, but it also exposes our worth.

"Therefore, since we have a great high priest who has ascended into heaven, Jesus the Son of God, let us hold firmly to the faith we profess. For we do not have a high priest who is unable to empathize with our weaknesses, but we have one who has been tempted in every way, just as we are—yet he did not sin. Let us then approach God's throne of grace with confidence, so that we may receive mercy and find grace to help us in our time of need."

Hebrews 4:14-16

The gospel is the good news that God who is holy and just, looked with grace and mercy on our sin, and in His great love sent His Son to proclaim and establish His Kingdom. Jesus came to sacrificially and selflessly die for us so that, by His death, resurrection and power, we could receive new and eternal life.

It is through Jesus that sin is forgiven, people are reconciled to God and the world will one day be made new. The gospel is the good news of Jesus and His Kingdom.

Entering into this relationship with Jesus is not based on anything we have done to earn God's approval or acceptance, but on everything Jesus did on our behalf to pay for our sin and bring us into His Kingdom.

"Now, brothers and sisters, I want to remind you of the gospel I preached to you, which you received and on which you have taken your stand. By this gospel you are saved, if you hold firmly to the word I preached to you. Otherwise, you have believed in vain. For what I received I passed on to you as of first importance: that Christ died for our sins according to the Scriptures, that he was buried, that he was raised on the third day according to the Scriptures."

1 Corinthians 15: 1-4

What does the word gospel mean?

_____

_____

THE KINGDOM OF GOD IN YOU

When someone enters into a relationship with God, the Kingdom of God comes into their life. The rule and reign of God and the power and presence of God made available in and through Christ dwells in them.

> *"To them God has chosen to make known among the Gentiles the glorious riches of this mystery, which is Christ in you, the hope of glory."*
>
> **Colossians 1:27**

> *"Don't you know that you yourselves are God's temple and that God's Spirit dwells in your midst?"*
>
> **Corinthians 3:16**

THE KINGDOM OF GOD IN THE FUTURE

It doesn't take much to look around at the world we live in and realize that although God's rule and reign has come into this world it is not yet fully governed by God's power and presence. The Kingdom has come to earth, but not in it's fullness. Scripture tells us there will come a day when Jesus the King will come back and when He does return He will fully set up His Kingdom. However, we learn in the book of Revelation that it will not be like the first time. The first time He came in humility, the second time He will come in glory. The first time He came in poverty, the second time He will come in power. The first time He came and suffered, the second time He will come in victory and triumph.

> *"Then I saw "a new heaven and a new earth," for the first heaven and the first earth had passed away, and there was no longer any sea. I saw the Holy City, the New Jerusalem, coming down out of heaven from God, prepared as a bride beautifully dressed for her husband. And I heard a loud voice from the throne saying, "Look! God's dwelling place is now among the*

people, and he will dwell with them. They will be his people, and God himself will be with them and be their God. 'He will wipe every tear from their eyes. There will be no more death' or mourning or crying or pain, for the old order of things has passed away." He who was seated on the throne said, "I am making everything new!" Then he said, "Write this down, for these words are trustworthy and true."

Revelation 21:1-5

"And this gospel of the kingdom will be preached in the whole world as a testimony to all nations, and then the end will come."

Matthew 24:14

What does it mean that the Kingdom of God has come, but not yet fully?

_____

_____

This is the story of the King and His Kingdom. It is the story of the rule and reign of God, the power and presence of God made available and accessible through the person of Jesus.

the KINGDOM STORY

KINGDOM IN THE GARDEN

KINGDOM THROUGH ISRAEL

KINGDOM IN THE TENT

KINGDOM IN THE TEMPLE

KINGDOM PROPHECY & SILENCE

THE KING & KINGDOM COMES

KINGDOM IN YOU

A NEW HEAVEN & NEW EARTH

LOOKING AT WHAT YOU LEARNED

Fill in the blanks below:

The Kingdom of God came first in the _____.

The Kingdom of God then came through the _____
to Abraham.

The Kingdom of God was in the _____
in the wilderness.

The Kingdom of God was in the _____
built by Solomon.

The Kingdom of God was prophesied about by the
_____.

The Kingdom of God finally came through the King of Kings
_____ in the New Testament.

The Kingdom of God will fully come when Jesus comes back
the _____ time.

TAKING TIME TO REFLECT FURTHER

How has this chapter contributed toward your understanding of
God and His desire for your life?

How did this help you understand the story of the Bible?

Did you have any questions after reading this chapter?

RECOMMENDED FURTHER RESOURCES

The Gospel of the Kingdom by George Eldon Ladd

The Kingdom of God by Martyn Llyod Jones

How God Became King by N.T. Wright

This Beautiful Mess: Practicing the Presence of the Kingdom of God by Rick McKinely and Donald Miller

The King Jesus Gospel by Scot McKnight

King's Cross: The Story and the World in the Life of Jesus by Tim Keller

The Story: The Bible as One Story of God and His People by Max Lucado and Randy Freeze

Gospel: Recovering the Power that Made Christianity Revolutionary by J.D. Greear and Tim Keller

The Gospel at the Center by D.A. Carson

Vintage Jesus by Mark Driscoll

Systematic Theology by Wayne Grudem

Knowing God by J.I. Packer

MY ASSIGNMENT FOR THIS WEEK IS:

NOTES

NOTES

PART 2:
SALVATION
IN THE KINGDOM

PART 2:
SALVATION

After we understand the story of the King, it is important to turn our attention toward what has taken place in our lives since we put our faith and hope in Jesus. When we trust in Jesus as our Savior and enter into His Kingdom, we experience salvation. Salvation is best defined as God's rescue of humanity from the consequences of sin resulting in a personal relationship with Jesus Christ and His Kingdom, for both now and all eternity. We are created, designed, and fashioned for eternity. We will either face an eternity with God, what the writers of scripture call Heaven or we will face an eternity without God, what the writers of scripture call Hell.

THE COST AND POWER OF SIN

Scripture makes it clear that every person is born into this world with a spiritual condition inherited from the first man and the first woman that separates us from a relationship with a Holy God. This spiritual condition is what the Bible refers to over and over again as sin.

"Surely I was sinful at birth, sinful from the time my mother conceived me."

Psalm 51:5

"For all have sinned and fall short of the glory of God."
Romans 3:23

Sin is anything that is not God's will for our lives. It is both a spiritual condition and an intentional choice. Whenever we choose not to let God rule and reign in our life, not to live by His power and presence, we choose to sin. Sin always brings separation, division, and death.

"For the wages of sin is death, but the gift of God is eternal life in Christ Jesus our Lord."
Romans 6:23

What is sin and what does it accomplish in our life?

_____

_____

Despite our sin, it is God's desire to have a personal relationship with us and establish His Kingdom in our life. We did not pursue God. God by His grace, mercy, and love pursued us.

FORGIVENESS FROM SIN

God's loving response to our rebellion and sin was to send His Son to rescue us from our sinful condition. Jesus, who was both God and man, lived a sinless life, healed the hurting, forgave sin, demonstrated the Kingdom of God, and died on a cross to become the complete sacrifice for our sin. Jesus not only died to pay for our sin, but He also rose victoriously from the grave three days later. Jesus is not just a good moral teacher, an inspiring guide, a prophet, or a wonder-working miracle maker.

Jesus is the Son of God, the Savior of the world and the King of Kings.

"For God so loved the world that He gave His one and only Son, that whoever believes in Him will not perish but have eternal life."

John 3:16

"But God demonstrated his own love for us in this: While we were still sinners, Christ died for us."

Romans 5:8

"The Son is the image of the invisible God, the firstborn over all creation. For in him all things were created: things in heaven and on earth, visible and invisible, whether thrones or powers or rulers or authorities; all things have been created through him and for him. He is before all things, and in him all things hold together. And he is the head of the body, the church; he is the beginning and the firstborn from among the dead, so that in everything he might have the supremacy. For God was pleased to have all his fullness dwell in him, and through him to reconcile to himself all things, whether things on earth or things in heaven, by making peace through his blood, shed on the cross."

Colossians 1:15-20

> **Salvation can never be earned, it can only be received. Salvation is a gift from God**

What did God do to resolve our sin problem?

_____

_____

_____

Why is it important to have a correct understanding of Jesus?

_____

_____

ADOPTION INTO GOD'S FAMILY

The truth is we cannot rescue ourselves from our sinful condition. Good intentions and New Year's resolutions are ineffective to deal with our spiritual brokenness. Try as we may, we always fall short. We can never make ourselves good enough to deserve God's love, and we can't do enough good things to cover up our sin and shame. Religious rituals and rules are ineffective to resolve the problem of our separation from God. The real problem of our sinful condition stems from something inside us, not from something outside of us. We need a rescuer, a Savior. The good news of the Kingdom is that Jesus Christ died for our sins. He died to rescue us and bring the reality of God's Kingdom into our lives.

What are some things that people do to try to make themselves right with God?

_____

_____

Salvation can never be earned. It can only be received. Salvation is a gift from God. We are saved when we trust in Jesus and accept His sacrifice on the cross for us. When we confess with our mouth and believe in our hearts that Jesus is Lord and Savior, we are saved. We are saved by faith alone, through faith alone, in Jesus alone. It is Jesus plus nothing that equals everything for us in Christ. When we give our lives to Jesus, we receive forgiveness for our sins and become adopted into God's family.

"If you declare with your mouth, "Jesus is Lord," and believe in your heart that God raised him from the dead, you will be saved. For it is with your heart that you believe and are justified, and it is with your mouth that you profess your faith and are saved."

Romans 10:9-10

"Yet to all who received him, to those who believed in his name, he gave the right to become children of God."

1 John 1:12

"For it is by grace you have been saved, through faith—and this is not from yourselves, it is the gift of God— not by works, so that no one can boast."

Ephesians 2:8-9

It is through Jesus that we receive salvation and the penalty of sin is completely removed from our life. However, this does not mean that we are not tempted to sin or that sin no longer has power in our life. Sin is a very real struggle for every follower of Jesus. After entering into a relationship with Jesus, we are still tempted to sin. The presence of sin continues, but through Jesus the power of sin is broken. We are now free to say "no" to sin and "yes" to God. We can and should take great comfort and joy in knowing that in Christ we have freedom and security.

"It is for freedom that Christ has set us free. Stand firm, then, and do not let yourselves be burdened again by a yoke of slavery."

Galatians 5:1

"And you also were included in Christ when you heard the message of truth, the gospel of your salvation. When you believed, you were marked in him with a seal, the promised Holy Spirit, who is a deposit guaranteeing our inheritance until the redemption of those who are God's possession — to the praise of his glory."

Ephesians 1:13-14

Is sin completely removed from our life after we experience salvation?

_____

_____

THE PROCESS OF SALVATION

As we grow in our relationship with God, there are some important concepts related to salvation that every follower of Jesus should know. These concepts give a brief and helpful explanation of what took place when we entered into a relationship with Jesus, what is taking place as we walk with Jesus and what will take place in the future as God's Kingdom is fully established.

"And we know that in all things God works for the good of those who love him, who have been called according to his purpose. For those God foreknew he also predestined to be conformed to the image of his Son, that he might be the firstborn among many brothers and sisters. And those he predestined, he also called; those he called, he also justified; those he justified, he also glorified."

Romans 8:28-30

REGENERATION

The process of salvation starts with regeneration. Regeneration is an act of God in which He spiritually awakens us to be able to put our trust and hope in Him. It is as if God turns on the light bulb of our heart and for the first time, we are sensitive and aware of God and His Kingdom.

"As for you, you were dead in your transgressions and sins, in which you used to live when you followed the ways of this world and of the ruler of the kingdom of the air, the spirit who is now at work in those who are disobedient. All of us also lived among them at one time, gratifying the cravings of our flesh[a] and following its desires and thoughts. Like the rest, we were by nature deserving of wrath. But because of his great love for us, God, who is rich in mercy, made us alive with Christ even when we were dead in transgressions—it is by grace you have been saved."

Ephesians 2:1-5

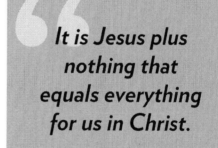

It is Jesus plus nothing that equals everything for us in Christ.

CONVERSION

The next step in the process of salvation is conversion. Conversion is our willing response to the gospel, where we repent of our sins and place our trust in Christ alone for salvation.

"If we confess our sins, he is faithful and just and will forgive us our sins and purify us from all unrighteousness."

1 John 1:9

JUSTIFICATION

Justification is an act of God whereby He fully forgives us of our sin and declares us righteous in His sight. We are now able to stand before a Holy God, not based on what we have done, but based on what Jesus did for us. An easy way to think of justification is to think of it this way: just as if we have never sinned. We are now justified in God's sight; whereas before we were lost and condemned by the penalty of sin. Justification is both instantaneous and irreversible.

> *"This righteousness is given through faith in Jesus Christ to all who believe. There is no difference between Jew and Gentile, for all have sinned and fall short of the glory of God, and all are justified freely by his grace through the redemption that came by Christ Jesus."*
>
> **Romans 3:22-24**

SANCTIFICATION

The next step in the process of salvation is called sanctification. Sanctification is the progressive and cooperative work of God in which we are conformed more and more into the image of Jesus. Justification happens instantaneously at the moment of our salvation, but sanctification is an ongoing work of God in our lives.

> *"Therefore, I urge you, brothers and sisters, in view of God's mercy, to offer your bodies as a living sacrifice, holy and pleasing to God—this is your true and proper worship. Do not conform to the pattern of this world, but be transformed by the renewing of your mind. Then you will be able to test and approve what God's will is—his good, pleasing and perfect will."*
>
> **Romans 12:1-2**

GLORIFICATION

The last and final step in the process of salvation is glorification. Glorification is what takes place when God's Kingdom is fully established on earth. Those who have entered into a relationship with God will spend eternity with God and receive a resurrected body.

> "Dear friends, now we are children of God, and what we will be has not yet been made known. But we know that when Christ appears, we shall be like him, for we shall see him as he is."
>
> **1 John 3:2**

The amazing gift of salvation we enjoy through Jesus Christ is absolutely incredible and life changing. The reality of our salvation should motivate us to worship God and live our lives for His glory. We do not live for God to earn His acceptance and approval, we live for God because in Christ we are accepted and approved. We do not live for God to earn His forgiveness and love, we live for God because in Christ we are fully forgiven and fully loved.

Write down the process of salvation in your own words.

_____

_____

_____

JESUS CHRIST

JESUS IS OUR SAVIOR

Jesus is not a savior, He is the savior. Jesus is not a good addition to our life. He did not come to give us good advice. Jesus came to save us, to rescue us and to deliver us into His Kingdom. Jesus did for us what we could not do for ourselves. Salvation is found in Jesus and Jesus alone. It is Jesus plus nothing that equals salvation for us. Acts 4:12

JESUS IS OUR HEALER

Jesus is our healer. The truth is that we want pleasure, we want power, we want joy, but we don't want pain and suffering. And yet it was through pain that we were brought into this word and our life is full of moments of suffering. Jesus does not minimize our pain or moralize our suffering, but instead is present and powerfully at work. Jesus has the power to heal our sicknesses, emotions, and brokenness. He can supernaturally heal us from sickness, use doctors and medicine in the healing process, or give us the grace to glorify Him in the middle of our sickness. Jesus is our savior, our sanctifier, and our healer. Isaiah 53:5

JESUS IS OUR SANCTIFIER

Jesus did not just come to save us, Jesus also came to sanctify us. Sanctify means to be set apart from sin and set apart to God. Jesus did not just come to rescue us from our sin and bring us into a restored relationship with Himself, Jesus came to grow us and transform us into His image. Jesus came to sanctify us so that we will glorify God, grow in joy, and extend His Kingdom. 2 Peter 1:3

JESUS IS OUR COMING KING

Jesus is our savior, Jesus is our sanctifier, Jesus is our healer and Jesus is our coming king. The first time Jesus came, He came in humility. The second time He will come in glory. The first time Jesus came, He came in poverty, the second time He will come in power. The first time Jesus came, He came and suffered. The second time He will come in victory and triumph. Jesus is coming again! Mark 14:62

LOOKING AT WHAT YOU LEARNED

Fill in the blanks below:

Salvation is God's _____ of humanity from the _____ of sin and into a _____ relationship with Himself for both _____ and _____.

Salvation cannot be _____, it can only be _____.

We are saved from the _____ of sin, but sin still has _____ in our lives.

The process of salvation is as follows: _____, _____, _____, _____ and _____.

TAKING TIME TO REFLECT FURTHER

How has this chapter contributed toward your understanding of God and His desire for your life?

How did this help you understand what has happened in your life through salvation?

Did you have any questions after reading this chapter?

RECOMMENDED FURTHER RESOURCES

Explicit Gospel by Matt Chandler

Jesus + Nothing = Everything by Tullian Tchividjian

Grace by Max Lucado

Putting Amazing Back into Grace by Michael Horton

The Transforming Power of the Gospel by Jerry Bridges

What's so Amazing about Grace by Philip Yancey

Who is this Man by John Ortberg

Seeing and Savoring Jesus Christ by John Piper

The Case for Christ by Lee Strobel

The Fourfold Gospel by A.B. Simpson

Living the Cross Centered Life by C.J. Mahaney

MY ASSIGNMENT FOR THIS WEEK IS:

NOTES

NOTES

NOTES

PART 3:
BAPTISM
& BIBLE
IN THE KINGDOM

PART 3: BAPTISM & BIBLE

Now that we have a greater understanding of our new life in the Kingdom of God through salvation, we will take a closer look at baptism, which is the next step in our journey of following Jesus.

THE SIGNIFICANCE OF BAPTISM

The word baptism means immersion. Baptism is a public declaration to other believers and a watching world that a person is now a part of God's family. Baptism does not bring about salvation, nor is it a requirement for salvation. Instead it's an outward symbol of the inward transformation that has taken place through Jesus.

In baptism, a person expresses and identifies with this new life in Christ. When a person stands before others, they are identifying with the life of Jesus, when they are immersed in water, they are identifying with the death of Jesus. When they are raised from the water, they are identifying with the resurrection of Jesus.

Baptism truly is an opportunity to publicly declare Jesus as our King and His Kingdom as our new way of life.

> *"What shall we say, then? Shall we go on sinning so that grace may increase? By no means! We are those who have died to sin; how can we live in it any longer? Or don't you know that all of us who were baptized into Christ Jesus were baptized into his death? We were therefore buried with him through baptism into death in order that, just as Christ was raised from the dead through the glory of the Father, we too may live a new life."*
>
> **Romans 6:1-4**

Define in one sentence the purpose of baptism.

_____

_____

THE BAPTISM OF JESUS

The baptism of Jesus marked the inauguration of His public ministry. At the age of thirty, before starting His public ministry, He came to the Jordan River and was baptized. It was a moment of affirmation, fulfillment and declaration of God's Kingdom through His Son.

> *"Then Jesus came from Galilee to the Jordan to be baptized by John. But John tried to deter him, saying, "I need to be baptized by you, and do you come to me?" Jesus replied, "Let it be so now; it is proper for us to do this to fulfill all righteousness." Then John consented. As soon as Jesus was baptized, he went up out of the water. At that moment heaven was opened, and he saw the Spirit of God descending like a dove and alighting on him. And a voice from heaven said, "This is my Son, whom I love; with him I am well pleased."*
>
> **Matthew 3:13-17**

THE COMMAND OF JESUS

Not only was Jesus baptized, He also commanded everyone who would come after Him and trust in Him, to be baptized.

Baptism was far more than a suggestion of Jesus; it was act of gratitude and obedience. His last words to His disciples included instructions to baptize those who entered into His Kingdom and trusted Him as Savior.

> "Then Jesus came to them and said, "All authority in heaven and on earth has been given to me. Therefore go and make disciples of all nations, baptizing them in the name of the Father and of the Son and of the Holy Spirit, and teaching them to obey everything I have commanded you. And surely I am with you always, to the very end of the age."
>
> **Matthew 28:18-20**

What did you learn about the life and teachings of Jesus as it relates to baptism?

_____

_____

_____

_____

Baptism is a public declaration to other believers and a watching world that we are now a part of God's family.

THE PRACTICE OF BAPTISM

The practice of baptism is done in different ways at various churches. Some churches think it is important to baptize children, but scripture seems to indicate that baptism is a personal decision. It happens after someone receives salvation. It is with this in mind that we recommend for infants to be dedicated to God, instead of being baptized. Dedication is the process where a family publicly declares that they will teach their children about God and His Kingdom, while living as godly examples before them.

Some churches baptize people by sprinkling with water rather than full immersion. However, most people believe baptism from a biblical perspective is an event that takes place when someone is fully immersed in water. In the beginning of the early church, we see an example of this in the life of Philip, who baptized a man by full immersion.

"As they traveled along the road, they came to some water and the eunuch said, "Look, here is water. What can stand in the way of my being baptized?" And he gave orders to stop the chariot. Then both Philip and the eunuch went down into the water and Philip baptized him. When they came up out of the water, the Spirit of the Lord suddenly took Philip away, and the eunuch did not see him again, but went on his way rejoicing."

Acts 8:36-39

Lastly, some see baptism as an ongoing practice, but the Bible indicates baptism is a one-time event. It is not something that we need to do over and over throughout our lifetime.

What is the difference between baptism and baby dedication?

_____

_____

How many times does someone need to be baptized?

_____

_____

The practice of baptism is a bold personal decision to live for Jesus, and publicly declare that He is the Savior King. Baptism is an aspect of gratitude, worship, obedience, and public confession of faith.

Why should a follower of Jesus be baptized?

_____

_____

Now that we understand the practice of baptism in the life of a follower of Jesus, it is time to look at how we learn about God and His Kingdom.

THE BIBLE: GOD'S REVEALED WORDS TO US

The best way to learn and grow in our relationship with God and our understanding of His Kingdom is to spend time on a regular basis in the Bible. The Bible teaches us about the character of God, the Kingdom of God, and what it really means to be a follower of Jesus.

The Bible is God's Word to us and for us. God used ordinary men, inspired by the Holy Spirit, to bring about the final product known to us as the Bible. The stories that we read in the Bible are stories of God working in and through the lives of people all throughout history to establish His Kingdom.

The Bible was written over a period of 1500 years, by roughly 40 authors on 3 continents (Asia, Africa, and Europe), in 3 different languages (Hebrew, Aramaic and Greek). Although the composition of the Bible shows great diversity, the message of Bible shows great unity. The Bible is the unified story of God working throughout history to bring His Kingdom on earth. The Bible is unique in both it's message and it's authorship.

Here is what the Bible says about itself:

> "All Scripture is God-breathed and is useful for teaching, rebuking, correcting and training in righteousness, so that the servant of God may be thoroughly equipped for every good work."
>
> **2 Timothy 3:16:17**

"For the word of God is alive and active. Sharper than any double-edged sword, it penetrates even to dividing soul and spirit, joints and marrow; it judges the thoughts and attitudes of the heart."

Hebrews 4:12

"And we also thank God continually because, when you received the word of God, which you heard from us, you accepted it not as a human word, but as it actually is, the word of God, which is indeed at work in you who believe."

1 Thessalonians 2:1-3

"The law of the LORD is perfect, refreshing the soul. The statutes of the LORD are trustworthy, making wise the simple. The precepts of the LORD are right, giving joy to the heart. The commands of the LORD are radiant, giving light to the eyes. The fear of the LORD is pure, enduring forever. The decrees of the LORD are firm, and all of them are righteous. They are more precious than gold, than much pure gold; they are sweeter than honey, than honey from the honeycomb. By them your servant is warned; in keeping them there is great reward."

Psalm 19: 7-11

Not only is the Bible the inspired Word of God, but also everything in the Bible points us to the person of Jesus. Listen to what Jesus himself said about the Old Testament, after He rose from the dead and first appeared to a group of people.

"He said to them, "How foolish you are, and how slow to believe all that the prophets have spoken! Did not the Messiah have to suffer these things and then enter his glory?" And beginning with Moses and all the Prophets, he explained to them what was said in all the Scriptures concerning himself."

Luke 24:25-26

Everything in the Bible points to Jesus and His Kingdom. Nothing is more beneficial for us as a follower of Jesus than to grow in maturity by consistently reading and engaging with God's Word. No one understands us better than God and no one understands what we need to know better than God. God is wiser than any wise writer. God is more caring than any counselor. God is more creative than any poet or artist and what God says will be more useful to us than what anyone else in the universe has to say.

Charles Swindoll, the former seminary president and pastor put it this way, "News articles may inform us. Novels may inspire us. Poetry may enrapture us. But only the living, active Word of God can transform us."

What do we learn from the Bible?

_____

_____

_____

_____

> *The Bible teaches us about the character of God, the Kingdom of God and what it really means to be a follower of Jesus.*

What makes the Bible different than any other book?

_____

_____

THE STRUCTURE OF THE BIBLE

Now that we understand the purpose of God's Word, it is worth walking through the structure of God's Word. The Bible, which means books, is divided into two parts: the Old Testament and the New Testament. The Old Testament takes place before Jesus was born and the New Testament starts with the birth of Jesus. The word testament means covenant or agreement and is used to point to how God worked in one period of history as opposed to another period of history.

What do the words Bible and testament mean?

_____

_____

OLD TESTAMENT

The Old Testament is written in the Hebrew language and contains 39 books that are traditionally sorted into four main categories.

Five Books of Moses
(Genesis, Exodus, Leviticus, Numbers, Deuteronomy)

The first five books in the Old Testament are typically attributed to Moses. They tell about the beginning of the world, the beginning of mankind, the beginning of sin, the beginning of God's people, and the beginning of God's Kingdom on earth.

Twelve Books of History
(Joshua, Judges, Ruth, 1 and 2 Samuel, 1 and 2 Kings, 1 and 2 Chronicles, Ezra, Nehemiah, Esther)

In the first five books, we find out how everything begins and in the following twelve books, we find out the history of God's people as a nation. We learn about the Promise Land, the judges, the first kings, the temple and more.

Five Books of Poetry
(Job, Psalms, Proverbs, Ecclesiastes, Song of Songs)

In these five books, we discover the character of God and the humanity of man in and through a collection of poetry and prose. These books express emotion and heartache, pain and wisdom, while inviting you into a deeper relationship with God.

Seventeen Books of the Prophets

(Major: Isaiah, Jeremiah, Lamentations, Ezekiel, Daniel | Minor: Hosea, Joel, Amos, Obadiah, Jonah, Micah, Nahum, Habakkuk, Zephaniah, Haggai, Zechariah, Malachi)

In the last seventeen books of the Old Testament, we learn from a group of prophets. A prophet is someone who speaks on behalf of God to the people. The books of the prophets were written before, during, and after God's people were taken into exile. They are usually divided into major and minor prophets. The reason why they are separated into the category of major and minor prophets is not based on their importance, but rather the size of the book. The smaller books are called the minor prophets and the larger books are called the major prophets.

How many books are in the Old Testament and what is the structure of the Old Testament?

_____

_____

_____

NEW TESTAMENT

The New Testament is written primarily in the language of Greek, with splashes of Hebrew and Aramaic and contains 27 books that are traditionally sorted into four main categories.

The Four Gospels

(Matthew, Mark, Luke and John)

The first four books of the New Testament function as narratives on the life, teachings, death, and resurrection of Jesus. Each writer has a different perspective that helps us understand more about Jesus and the Kingdom He brings.

The Book of Acts

(Acts)

The book of Acts is the incredible story of the first followers of Jesus in the years directly following the resurrection and ascension of Jesus. It is the story of the early church.

The Epistles or Letters
(Romans, 1 and 2 Corinthians, Galatians, Ephesians, Philippians, Colossians, 1 and 2 Thessalonians, 1 and 2 Timothy, Titus, Philemon, Hebrews, James, 1 and 2 Peter, 1, 2 and 3 John, Jude)

These twenty-one books aren't really books at all. They are letters, most of which are written by a man named Paul. These letters were written to various churches going through various struggles. All of these letters help us understand what it means to live life in the Kingdom of God.

The Final Book: Revelation
(Revelation)

Revelation is the last book of the Bible. It describes, in prophetic detail, what will happen when God's Kingdom is fully established here on earth. It has spectacular imagery, scenes of war and scenes of peace.

How many books are in the New Testament and what is the structure of the New Testament?

_____

_____

_____

HOW TO READ THE BIBLE

Now that we have understood the purpose of the Bible and the structure of the Bible, it is time to look at reading the Bible. Here are some helpful suggestions.

PLACE, PLAN, AND TRANSLATION

If you are going to consistently learn from God's Word it helps to develop a plan. Begin with finding a suitable place to read and choose a reader-friendly translation. A great starting place to read is in the Gospels. You will understand scripture the best when you read about the life and teachings of Jesus. The perfect place is different for each person. The most important thing is to pick a place with minimal distractions. Last, but not least, selecting an easy to read translation will allow you to feel more at home in the Bible. It is worth investing in a good study Bible. Good translations to consider are the NIV or ESV. It is called a translation because a team of experts and scholars translated the Bible from Hebrew or Greek into English for us to read and enjoy.

OBSERVATION, INTERPRETATION AND APPLICATION

After you have developed a plan, picked a place, and selected a good translation, consider three helpful questions that will enable you to truly get the most out of your time in scripture.

Observation (What do I See?)

When you read through scripture, slow down to observe the details. The first question you should always ask is, "What do I see?" What is going on in the passage you are reading? Who are the main characters? What terms are used? What is God saying or doing? What is the context? It is important to slow down and take time to observe.

Interpretation (What does it Mean?)

After you have taken time to learn the context and observe the details, now you are ready to move on and find out the meaning of the passage. This is where a study Bible will be useful. It is worth taking time to use qualified sources to help you gain new insight into the meaning of scripture.

Application (How does this Apply?)

The last question you should ask is, "How does this apply to me?" Remember the purpose of reading scripture is not simply to gain new information, but to lead toward a greater transformation. It is not enough to just observe and interpret, we need to be people who apply God's word to our life.

Write down your place, plan, and chosen translation.

_____

_____

_____

Describe the difference between observation, interpretation, and application.

_____

_____

_____

LOOKING AT WHAT YOU LEARNED

Fill in the blanks below:

The word baptism means _____.

Baptism is not a _____ for salvation.

Baptism is a public _____ of the _____ transformation that has taken place in our life through Jesus.

The word Bible means _____. The word testament means _____.

The Old Testament was written in _____ and the New Testament was primarily written in _____.

TAKING TIME TO REFLECT FURTHER

How has this chapter contributed toward your understanding of God and His desire for your life?

How did this help you better understand baptism and the Bible?

Did you have any questions after reading this chapter?

RECOMMENDED FURTHER RESOURCES

How We Got the Bible by Neil Lightfoot

How to Read the Bible for All it's Worth by Gordon Fee

Living by the Book by Howard Hendricks

The Blue Parakeet by Scot McKnight

The Bible Jesus Read by Philip Yancey

How to Read the Bible through the Jesus lens by Michael Williams

Rick Warren's Bible Study Methods by Rick Warren

How to Study the Bible by John MacArthur

MY ASSIGNMENT FOR THIS WEEK IS:

NOTES

NOTES

NOTES

PART 4:
PRAYER &
COMMUNITY
IN THE KINGDOM

PART 4: PRAYER & COMMUNITY

As we grow in our relationship with God, it is important to understand that life in the Kingdom of God is all about relationships. The best way that people grow in any relationship is to spend time together and learn to communicate with each other. The same is true in our relationship with God. We will grow in our relationship with God as we spend time with God and learn to communicate with God.

WHAT IS PRAYER?

Prayer is simply communicating with God. It is a conversation with the God who loves us and invites us to talk with Him. Prayer is one of the most incredible blessings that God gives to us as His children. It's amazing to think that we are invited to talk with God! We learn about God through the Bible, but we communicate with God through prayer.

"Do not be anxious about anything, but in every situation, by prayer and petition, with thanksgiving, present your requests to God. And the peace of God, which transcends all understanding, will guard your hearts and your minds in Christ Jesus."

Philippians 4:6-7

What is prayer?

_____

_____

THE CHARACTER OF GOD

It is through prayer that we have the opportunity and invitation to talk with God. Since this is true, it is crucial for us to understand the character or attributes of God. How do we know He can answer our prayers? With this in mind we will walk through some of the characteristics or attributes of God. When we understand the character of God, we will approach God in prayer with courage and confidence.

GOD IS OMNISCIENT

God knows everything. He knows the past, the present, and the future. God knows all things technical and trivial. He knows us better than we even know ourselves. We can approach God in prayer with honesty because He already knows our heart.

"You have searched me, Lord, and you know me. You know when I sit and when I rise; you perceive my thoughts from afar. You discern my going out and my lying down; you are familiar with all my ways. Before a word is on my tongue you, Lord, know it completely."

Psalm 139:1-4

GOD IS OMNIPRESENT

God is everywhere. We cannot escape or hide from God. He is completely available and present. We can approach God in prayer with humility because He is ever-present in our life. He does not leave us or abandon us.

> "Where can I go from your Spirit? Where can I flee from your presence? If I go up to the heavens, you are there; if I make my bed in the depths, you are there."
>
> **Psalm 139:7-9**

GOD IS OMNIPOTENT

God is all-powerful. There is no person or people, country or military force that is more powerful than God. God is sovereign or in complete control. We can approach God in prayer with boldness because He not only hears our prayers, but also can answer our prayers. Nothing is too large for God to handle.

> "Ah, Sovereign Lord, you have made the heavens and the earth by your great power and outstretched arm. Nothing is too hard for you."

We learn about God through the Bible, but we communicate with God through prayer.

> **Jeremiah 32:17**

GOD IS IMMUTABLE

God doesn't change. His character is the same yesterday, today and forever. In a world that is always changing, we serve a God who never changes. We can approach God in prayer with confidence because He is consistent and faithful.

> "I the Lord do not change."
>
> **Malachi 3:6a**

GOD IS HOLY

God is a holy God. He is righteous and without fault. He is flawless in His moral character and void of any evil. We can approach God in prayer and expect to find a God who is pure and holy.

> "And they were calling to one another: "Holy, holy, holy is the Lord Almighty; the whole earth is full of his glory."
>
> **Isaiah 6:3**

GOD IS LOVE

God, by His very nature, is love. When we come to God, we can expect that He has our best interest in mind. God is for us for our joy and His glory. He does not sabotage our life or hold grudges against us. God loves us and wants what is best for us. We can approach God in prayer with vulnerability because He loves us.

> "Dear friends, let us love one another, for love comes from God. Everyone who loves has been born of God and knows God. Whoever does not love does not know God, because God is love."
>
> **1 John 4:7-8**

What are the six characteristics or attributes of God mentioned above? Which is hardest for you to understand?

_____

_____

_____

_____

HOW TO PRAY

Sometimes we have a distorted concept of prayer. We think of someone praying a beautiful prayer in public using a holy tone and big words. We feel like our prayer can't compare with theirs. But God is not interested in hearing a perfectly formed prayer. He wants you to talk with Him as you would talk with a friend. Transparency, humility, and honesty are essential qualities as we talk with God.

In Jesus' time there was a group of people called the Pharisees. They were a religious group that strictly followed the Jewish law and had added many traditions of their own. They prided themselves in their long beautiful public prayers and in obeying these additional religious rules. On several occasions Jesus referred to them as hypocrites. Read what Jesus says about their prayers:

> "And when you pray, do not be like the hypocrites, for they love to pray standing in the synagogues and on the street corners to be seen by others. Truly I tell you, they have received their reward in full... And when you pray, do not keep babbling like pagans, for they think they will be heard because of their many words."
>
> **Matthew 6:5,7**

Prayer has nothing to do with the amount of words we say, but everything to do with the condition of our heart. Prayer is not about saying the right words, it is about having the right heart attitude. Three characteristics of a healthy prayer life are transparency, humility and honesty. C.S. Lewis put it best, "We should bring to God what is in us, and not what we think should be in us."

What are three characteristics of a healthy prayer life?

_____

_____

KINGDOM PRAYER OR LORD'S PRAYER

We know that God invites us to pray, but we struggle at times with what to pray. We are not alone. On one occasion Jesus disciples approached Him and made this request, "Jesus, teach us how to pray." The disciples wanted to learn to pray like Jesus. At that time Jesus taught them the famous prayer called, the Lord's Prayer or the Kingdom Prayer. There are just sixty words in this prayer, but it is the most repeated prayer in history. Jesus gave this prayer as a model for the disciples and we have every reason to believe that they prayed this prayer more than any other prayer.

"This, then, is how you should pray: "'Our Father in heaven, hallowed be your name, your kingdom come, your will be done, on earth as it is in heaven. Give us today our daily bread. And forgive us our debts, as we also have forgiven our debtors. And lead us not into temptation, but deliver us from the evil one. For yours is the kingdom and the power and the glory forever. Amen."

Matthew 6:9-13

If we use the Lord's Prayer as a guide we can learn what to pray and specifically how to pray as followers of Jesus.

OUR FATHER

First, we address God personally. When we receive Jesus, we are adopted into God's family. He is now our Father. We begin talking with God by recognizing that He is a loving Father who wants to communicate with us.

HALLOWED BE YOUR NAME

Second, we talk to God respectfully. God expects us to come to Him with respect, recognizing that He is the Creator of the universe, the eternal God. God's name is to be hallowed. Hallowed is not a word we hear very often. The word hallowed means to consider something as holy or sacred.

YOUR KINGDOM COME

Third, we pray for God's Kingdom to come and for His will to be done on earth as it is in heaven. Each day as followers of Jesus we are invited by God to pray, "Your Kingdom on earth through me." In doing this we are praying that God's rule, reign, power and presence would take place in our life and through our life. We want His priorities to be our priorities and His agenda to be our agenda. We are asking God to help us bring His Kingdom into our relationships and all areas of influence.

OUR DAILY BREAD

Fourth, we are encouraged to ask God for what we need. God cares about us personally. He hears us when we pray and has promised to provide for our needs. Don't feel ashamed about asking God for specific needs in your life. Are you sick? Ask God for healing. Are you discouraged? Tell God how you feel. Just remember that God promises to give us what we need, not everything we want. Sometimes "no" or "not at this time" is the answer to our request.

> **When we glorify God, we truly become satisfied in Him. God is for us, for our joy and His glory.**

WE FORGIVE OTHERS

Fifth, we ask God to help us forgive those who have wronged us. Forgiveness is not natural to us. Yet God makes it clear that if we want to be forgiven we must be willing to forgive others. When we think about Jesus dying on the cross for our sins we realize how much we have been forgiven. We are to forgive others just like God forgave us. Forgiveness doesn't mean we can forget what took place in our lives, but it does mean we choose not to hold their offenses against them any longer.

DELIVER US

Sixth, we ask God to help us say "no" to sin. As we pray we should confess our sins to God and ask Him to help us overcome temptations. We should also acknowledge that living like Jesus is difficult for us. In our prayers, we are asking God to help us say "no" to sin as we go throughout our day.

ALL FOR THE GLORY OF GOD

Finally, we end our prayers by worshipping the King and giving all glory to Him. In every area of our life, we want to glorify God. When we glorify God, we truly become satisfied in Him. Every circumstance presents an opportunity to glorify God.

> *"Whatever you do, work at it with all your heart, as working for the Lord, not for human masters."*
> **Colossians 3:23**

> *"So whether you eat or drink or whatever you do, do it all for the glory of God."*
> **1 Corinthians 10:31**

What part of the Lord's Prayer is the most difficult for you to pray? What part is the easiest?

_____

_____

_____

Now that we understand what to pray and how to pray, it is time to look at learning to live in community with others. We may enter into a relationship with God alone, but we were never meant or called to grow in our relationship with God alone.

COMMUNITY IN THE KINGDOM

Life in the Kingdom is all about relationships with God and with others. We are not alone and this is good news! When we enter the Kingdom of God we become part of God's family. There are others who have made the same decision to follow Jesus and they are also part of the family. In our relationship with God, we should not struggle alone, celebrate alone, worship alone, learn alone, or grow alone. In healthy biblical community we are friends on a mission. A mission to glorify God and to build His Kingdom.

> "Yet to all who receive him (Jesus), to those who believed in his name, he gave the right to become children of God."
>
> **John 1:12**

> "Because we loved you so much, we were delighted to share with you not only the gospel of God but our lives as well."
>
> **1 Thessalonians 2:7**

CREATED FOR COMMUNITY

We are created by God and for God and created to live life in community with others. We are intentionally and purposefully wired to relate to others. In fact, Jesus commanded his followers to love each other.

> "A new commandment I give to you, that you love one another, even as I have loved you, that you also love one another."
>
> **John 13:34**

When we love each other, we challenge each other, care for each other, support each other, pray for each other, and encourage each other.

> "Therefore encourage one another and build up one another, just as you also are doing."
>
> **1 Thessalonians 5:11**

Jesus prays for those who would come after Him directly before His death. He prays that they would exhibit the same type of humility, transparency, and selflessness that exists inside of the relationship between the Father and the Son.

> *"My prayer is not for them alone. I pray also for those who will believe in me through their message, that all of them may be one, Father, just as you are in me and I am in you. May they also be in us so that the world may believe that you have sent me."*
> **John 17:20-21**

It is not a mistake that we crave community. Community is at the very heart of life in the Kingdom. We are created for community and anytime we live life outside of community we are missing out on what God has called us to be and to do.

GATHERED IN A NEW COMMUNITY

The community that God created and gathered to extend His Kingdom on earth through Jesus is called the church. When we think of the word church, thoughts and images flood into our mind.

We may think of buildings, many types of worship songs, programs and styles of preaching. Yet in a biblical sense, the word church is a term that refers not to a building or style of music or a specific type of program or a denomination. The word church refers to a community of people who have given their life to Jesus and entered into His Kingdom.

There is a big difference between the expressions of the church and the church itself. There might be many expressions of the church, but there is only one church. As followers of Jesus, who have given our life to Him, we do not go to church as much as we are a new community called the church. The word church means, a called out people or community. When Jesus talks to Peter, He instructs him that He will build this new community and nothing will overcome it.

"And I tell you that you are Peter, and on this rock I will build my church, and the gates of Hades will not overcome it."
Matthew 16:18

Everyone who receives Jesus, as their Savior is part of this new community called the church. The church is far from perfect, but nevertheless is a family. Like any family, we should gather together, pray for each other, encourage one another, support each other, and grow in maturity together.

"And let us consider how we may spur one another on toward love and good deeds, not giving up meeting together, as some are in the habit of doing, but encouraging one another – and all the more as you see the day approaching."
Hebrews 10:25

What is the church?

_____

_____

Why is living in community with others so important?

_____

_____

LOOKING AT WHAT YOU LEARNED

Fill in the blanks below:

Prayer is _____ to God.

When we pray, we should pray with _____ and
_____.

Jesus gave us an example of what to pray and how to pray in the
_____.

We are created by God and created to live in
_____ with other people.

The word church means _____
____.

TAKING TIME TO REFLECT FURTHER

How has this chapter contributed toward your understanding of
God and His desire for your life?

How did this help you better understand prayer and community?

Did you have any questions after reading this chapter?

RECOMMENDED FURTHER RESOURCES

Prayer by Philip Yancey

The Pursuit of God by A.W. Tozer

The Prayer of the Lord by R. C. Sproul

Too Busy Not to Pray by Bill Hybels

The Essentials of Prayer by E.M. Bounds

Prayer: Finding the Heart's True Home by Richard Foster

Emotionally Healthy Spirituality by Pete Scazzero

Community by Brad House

True Community by Jerry Bridges

Everybody is Normal Until You Get to Know Them by John Ortberg

MY ASSIGNMENT FOR THIS WEEK IS:

NOTES

NOTES

PART 5:
GROWTH
& POWER
IN THE KINGDOM

PART 5: GROWTH & POWER

As we continue our journey in God's Kingdom, we can expect great things to happen in our spiritual lives. It's exciting to understand that God's Kingdom is not passive. It is continually advancing. As we are responsive to Jesus, we will see growth and change in our lives.

Jesus shared two parables in the book of Matthew that give us some helpful imagery to understand the dynamic growth of the Kingdom of God. A parable is a fictional story that teaches a factual spiritual truth.

STARTING SMALL
The Parable of the Mustard Seed

> *"He told them another parable: The kingdom of heaven is like a mustard seed, which a man took and planted in his field. Though it is the smallest of all seeds, yet when it grows, it is the largest of garden plants and becomes a tree, so that the birds come and perch in its branches."*
>
> **Matthew 13: 31-32**

This parable illustrates the truth that The Kingdom of God may start off small in our lives, but as we respond to God it becomes large. We often enter God's Kingdom with issues and baggage. Sometimes God produces instant change as we put our faith, hope, and trust in Jesus. At other times it is a process of change that starts small, but grows, and spreads. We should never discount the small beginnings of our lives. The small decisions make the big difference. As we respond in faith and obedience to Jesus we can expect the Kingdom of God to grow in our life and change our character, perspective and passions.

ALWAYS WORKING
The Parable of the Leaven

> *"He told them still another parable: "The Kingdom of heaven is like yeast that a woman took and mixed into about sixty pounds of flour until it worked all through the dough."*
>
> **Matthew 13:33**

When we eat bread we seldom think of yeast. Why? Because we don't see it, but the yeast makes it possible to bake bread that is soft and delicious. It only takes a little, but as yeast ferments, the bread rises. A small amount of yeast silently produces a large effect. In the parable, Jesus is reminding us that many times the Kingdom of God is producing changes in our lives that we don't see. As we consistently yield to God's work in our lives, He is in the process of changing us to become more like Jesus. As we nurture God's Word and foster obedience, we can expect to see growth and changes. It is Christ in us that makes all the difference to us. The gospel of the Kingdom of God is always at work in the life of believers.

> *"That has come to you. In the same way, the gospel is bearing fruit and growing throughout the whole world—just as it has been doing among you since the day you heard it and truly understood God's grace."*
>
> **Colossians 1:6**

"And we know that in all things God works for the good of those who love him, who have been called according to his purpose."

Romans 8:28

God's Kingdom should be advancing in our lives daily. Spiritual growth and maturity are both a work of God and partnership with God. While salvation is a free gift that does not come to us through our efforts, spiritual growth and maturity in the Kingdom is the result of God's effort and our cooperation. When we pursue God and His Kingdom we will be amazed at how God helps us to mature and grow.

What do these two parables teach us about the growth of the Kingdom?

_____

_____

_____

_____

> **All of our efforts to move forward in spiritual maturity must be grounded in grace.**

DRIVEN BY GRACE

It is important to know that growth in the Kingdom of God is driven by the grace of God. The very same grace that brings us into salvation is also the grace that is instrumental in training us to live the Christian life. All of our efforts to move forward in spiritual maturity must be grounded in grace. God cares about our obedience, but He also cares about our motives behind the obedience. When we are motivated and driven by the grace of God, we are mindful that it is not about our performance, but about Christ performance for us. We are dearly and deeply loved by God and by God's grace, we become more fully devoted followers of Jesus.

"For the grace of God has appeared that offers salvation to all people. It teaches us to say "No" to ungodliness and worldly passions, and to live self-controlled, upright and godly lives in this present age."

Titus 2:11-12

THE HOLY SPIRIT

The Holy Spirit is the source of power in the Kingdom of God. When a person receives Jesus Christ as Savior he becomes a follower, a disciple of Jesus. Following His resurrection Jesus ascended to heaven and according to the Bible, is seated at the right hand of God the Father. Before He ascended Jesus promised that He would send the Holy Spirit to be with His followers. The moment a person receives Jesus the Holy Spirit comes into their life. This not only makes us a child of God, but also provides us with confidence and strength. The Holy Spirit enables us to live the Christian life.

Who is the Holy Spirit? The Holy Spirit is the third person of the Trinity. He is God. Although the word trinity is not used in the Bible, the concept of one God existing in three persons is clearly taught in many passages in the Bible.

"Then Jesus came to them and said, 'All authority in heaven and earth has been given to me. Therefore go and make disciples of all nations, baptizing them in the name of the Father and of the Son and of the Holy Spirit."

Matthew 28:18-19

"May the grace of the Lord Jesus Christ, and the love of God, and the fellowship of the Holy Spirit be with you all."

2 Corinthians 13:14

In the New Testament we learn some important truths about the Holy Spirit.

THE HOLY SPIRIT IS PERSONAL

The Holy Spirit is a person, not a thing. Some religions teach that the Holy Spirit is a spiritual force that flows through the world. The Bible always refers to the Holy Spirit with the pronoun, "He". We relate to the Holy Spirit as we relate to a person.

> *"If you love me, keep my commands. And I will ask the Father, and he will give you another advocate to help you and be with you forever – the Spirit of truth. The world cannot accept him, because it neither sees him nor knows him. But you know him, for he lives with you and will be in you."*
>
> **John 14:15-17**

THE HOLY SPIRIT IS GOD

> *"Then Peter said, 'Ananias, how is it that Satan has so filled your heart that you have lied to the Holy Spirit…You have not lied just to human beings but to God."*
>
> **Acts 5: 3-4**

THE HOLY SPIRIT LIVES IN US

> *"You, however are controlled not by the sinful nature but by the Spirit, if the Spirit of God lives in you. And if anyone does not have the Spirit of Christ, he does not belong to Christ."*
>
> **Romans 8: 8-9**

THE HOLY SPIRIT GLORIFIES AND GUIDES

"But when he, the Spirit of truth, comes, He will guide you into all truth… He will bring glory to me by taking from what is mine and making it known to you."

John 16:13-14

THE HOLY SPIRIT TEACHES AND COMFORTS

"All this I have spoken while still with you. But the Advocate the Holy Spirit, whom the Father will send in my name, will teach you all things and will remind you of everything I have said to you."

John 14:25- 26

THE HOLY SPIRIT GIVES SPIRITUAL GIFTS

As Christ followers it's amazing to understand that God lives in us and is available daily to help us grow in God's Kingdom! The Holy Spirit empowers us to say "no" to sin and "yes" to life in God's Kingdom.

One way that the Holy Spirit equips us to participate in God's Kingdom is by giving us spiritual gifts. A spiritual gift is a special ability that the Holy Spirit gives to every believer to bless the Kingdom community and impact the world.

"We have different gifts, according to the grace given to each of us. If your gift is prophesying, then prophesy in accordance with your faith; if it is serving, then serve; if it is teaching, then teach; if it is to encourage, then give encouragement; if it is giving, then give generously; if it is to lead, do it diligently; if it is to show mercy, do it cheerfully."

Romans 12:6-8

"There are different kinds of gifts, but the same Spirit distributes them. There are different kinds of service, but the same Lord. There are different kinds of working, but in all of them and in everyone it is the same God at work."

1 Corinthians 12:4-6

"Each of you should use whatever gift you have received to serve others, as faithful stewards of God's grace in its various forms. If anyone speaks, they should do so as one who speaks the very words of God. If anyone serves, they should do so with the strength God provides, so that in all things God may be praised through Jesus Christ. To him be the glory and the power for ever and ever. Amen."

1 Peter 4:10-11

Here are some things that are clear as we look at what scripture has to say about spiritual gifts.

> **The Holy Spirit empowers us to live life in the Kingdom and experience God's rule and reign.**

1.) Every believer receives at least one gift.

2.) The gifts are given to strengthen the church and to impact the world.

3.) The Holy Spirit is the giver of the gifts and He gives each person the gifts He chooses.

4.) The gifts should be exercised with humility and love. Spiritual gifts are intended to serve people and bring God glory. They are not intended to make us proud or feel superior to others.

Understanding our spiritual gifts is a process. This process includes studying the Bible, praying for revelation from the Holy Spirit, and seeking confirmation from friends.

Why does the Holy Spirit give us spiritual gifts?

_____

_____

THE HOLY SPIRIT EMPOWERS US TO WIN SPIRITUAL BATTLES

The Bible is clear that when a person becomes a follower of Jesus they are delivered from the power of sin, given a new life in Christ, and have authority over spiritual forces. Every believer must recognize that they are in a spiritual battle. Satan is the enemy and seeks to distract and attack those who are part of God's Kingdom. The Bible teaches that Satan was defeated by Jesus on the cross. He has no authority over the believer who is in Christ. It is through the empowerment of the Holy Spirit that we resist the enemy and stand strong in moments of spiritual opposition.

> *"Put on the full armor of God so that you can take your stand against the devil's scheme. For our struggle is not against flesh and blood, but against the rulers, against the authorities, against the powers of this dark world and against the spiritual forces of evil in the heavenly realms. Therefore put on the full armor of God, so that when the day of evil comes, you may be able to stand your ground, and after you have done everything to stand."*
>
> **Ephesians 6:11-13**

THE HOLY SPIRIT FILLS US AND PRODUCES FRUIT

God lives in us and wants to give us all we need to live for Him each day. The Holy Spirit doesn't just encourage us, but desires to fill us. The word fill doesn't refer to quantity, but instead refers to control. As we give the Holy Spirit control of every area of our lives He empowers us to live life in the Kingdom and experience God's rule and reign.

"Do not get drunk on wine, which leads to debauchery. Instead, be filled with the Spirit."

Ephesians 5:18

There are several obstacles to being controlled by the Holy Spirit. One is our natural desire to control our own lives. As we get to know God, we begin to see that He does a much better job of directing our lives than we do. We must come to the point of wanting the Holy Spirit to be in control.

Another obstacle is allowing sin to remain in our lives. As we confess our sin, the Holy Spirit is free to work powerfully in and through us.

We should come daily to God in prayer and ask the Holy Spirit to fill us. As we give control of our lives to the Holy Spirit, He produces certain qualities in us that are consistent with Kingdom living. These qualities are referred to as the fruit of the Spirit.

"But the fruit of the Spirit is love, joy, peace, patience, kindness, goodness, faithfulness, gentleness and self-control."

Galatians 5:22-23a

We can expect to see greater evidence of the fruit of the Spirit, as we grow closer to Jesus. Throughout our spiritual lives we should be asking, "Is the fruit of the Spirit more evident in my life now than it was when I first started my journey in the Kingdom?" God is in the business of making us more like Christ. May the evidence of the fruit of the Spirit be overflowing in our lives as we move forward extending the Kingdom of God.

LOOKING AT WHAT YOU LEARNED

Fill in the blanks below:

The Kingdom of God is like a _____ seed. It starts _____, but grows _____.

The Kingdom of God is like _____. We may not be able to _____ everything, but that doesn't mean God is not _____.

The Holy Spirit is _____.

The Holy Spirit gives us spiritual _____.

The Holy Spirit _____ us to live in the Kingdom.

TAKING TIME TO REFLECT FURTHER

How has this chapter contributed toward your understanding of God and His desire for your life?

How did this help you better understand growing in God's Kingdom?

How did this help you understand more about the power of the Kingdom?

Did you have any questions after reading this chapter?

RECOMMENDED FURTHER RESOURCES

The Forgotten God by Francis Chan

How to Be Filled by the Holy Spirit by A.W. Tozer

Renovation of the Heart by Dallas Willard

Radical by David Platt

Mere Christianity by C.S. Lewis

Ruthless Trust by Brennan Manning

Desiring God by John Piper

Soul Detox by Craig Groeschel

The Holy Spirit by Billy Graham

Greater by Steven Furtick

Experiencing the Spirit by Henry Blackaby

Keep in Step with the Spirit by J.I. Packer

MY ASSIGNMENT FOR THIS WEEK IS:

NOTES

NOTES

PART 6:
COMMAND &
COMMISSION
IN THE KINGDOM

PART 6:
COMMAND &
COMMISSION

After learning about where our power comes from its time to focus on the central command and commission that drives and directs our life in the Kingdom of God.

KINGDOM COMMAND

There are 613 commandments found in the Old Testament. In the time of Jesus, most Jewish people not only attempted to memorize these laws, but also attempted to live by them. It was often debated among people which command was the greatest to follow. At one point a curious religious leader came to Jesus and asked Him out of all the commands, "which one is the greatest?" Jesus replied and in His reply gave us the Kingdom command.

> *"The most important one," answered Jesus, "is this: 'Hear, O Israel: The Lord our God, the Lord is one. Love the Lord your God with all your heart and with all your soul and with all your mind and with all your strength. The second is this: 'Love your*

neighbor as yourself.' There is no commandment greater than these."

Mark 12:29-31

In a few words, Jesus laid out the foundation for being a disciple. A disciple is commanded to display an upward love, inward love, and outward love. Surprisingly, it doesn't start with our actions or our knowledge, but rather our love.

AN UPWARD LOVE: LOVING GOD

Loving God is the greatest command in the entire Bible. This is not a casual love like our love for sports or food. This is a deeply committed and surrendered love for the creator and sustainer of life. It is out of this love that we pursue His Kingdom.

"But seek first the kingdom of God and his righteousness, and all these things will be added to you."

Matthew 6:33

"The kingdom of heaven is like treasure hidden in a field, which a man found and covered up. Then in his joy he goes and sells all that he has and buys that field."

Matthew 13:44

God wants and deserves to be our highest desire. He wants us to love Him above all else, to know Him better than we know anyone else, and His Kingdom to be our greatest pursuit. The Kingdom command is to love God above all things.

What is the greatest command in the Bible?

_____

_____

AN INWARD LOVE: LOVING YOURSELF

Another part of this Kingdom command is not only to love God, but also to show love to ourselves. It is only out of our love for God that we are truly able to love others and ourselves. Loving ourself is one of the most difficult challenges in our spiritual formation. As our love for God deepens, we discover our true identity. We are loved sons and daughters of the King.

"But God demonstrates his own love for us in this: While we were still sinners, Christ died for us."

Romans 5:6-8

"But you are a chosen race, a royal priesthood, a holy nation, a people for his own possession, that you may proclaim the excellencies of him who called you out of darkness into His marvelous light. Once you were not a people, but now you are God's people; once you had not received mercy, but now you have received mercy."

> **God wants us to love Him above all else, to know Him better than we know anyone else, and His Kingdom to be our greatest pursuit.**

1 Peter 2:9-10

"For we are God's handiwork, created in Christ Jesus to do good works, which God prepared in advance for us to do."

Ephesians 2:10

God has created us in His image and adopted us into His family. Therefore we are children of God and He loves us. It is out of our identity in Christ that we are able to love others and ourselves.

How do we come to the point of really loving ourselves?

_____

_____

AN OUTWARD LOVE: LOVING OTHERS

We are commanded to love God, to love ourselves, and to love others. Love is one of the most important character traits that should mark our lives as followers of Jesus.

> "And now these three remain: faith, hope and love. But the greatest of these is love."
>
> **1 Corinthians 13:13**

> "We love because he first loved us. If anyone says, "I love God," and hates his brother, he is a liar; for he who does not love his brother whom he has seen cannot love God whom he has not seen. And this commandment we have from him: whoever loves God must also love his brother."
>
> **1 John 4:19-21**

It is impossible to love God and not love others. Contrary to popular thought, we don't love others simply through service, but also in how we treat one another. Our love for others should impact how we treat everyone: believer or not, rich or poor, man or woman, old or young.

> "A new commandment I give to you, that you love one another: just as I have loved you, you also are to love one another. By this all people will know that you are my disciples, if you have love for one another."
>
> **John 13:35**

Which types of people are difficult for you to love? Which types of people are easy for you to love?

_____

_____

KINGDOM COMMISSION

Now that we have explored the Kingdom command, we will look at what is called the Kingdom commission. Jesus not only gave us a central command, He also gave us a central commission. This commission is found in the last words Jesus said to His disciples before being taken up to heaven.

> *"And Jesus came and said to them, "All authority in heaven and on earth has been given to me. Go therefore and make disciples of all nations, baptizing them in the name of the Father and of the Son and of the Holy Spirit, teaching them to observe all that I have commanded you. And behold, I am with you always, to the end of the age."*
>
> **Matthew 28:18-20**

The Kingdom commission of Jesus is a vision for discipleship. Discipleship is not a one time event, it is a lifelong journey. Discipleship is not just for new believers in Christ, it is for every believer in Christ. It is not an optional part of the Christian life, it is an essential part of the Christian life. Discipleship is the process of becoming a fully devoted follower of Jesus.

Let's examine a couple of key words from the commission Jesus gave and their impact on our life as His followers.

ALL AUTHORITY

The Kingdom commission begins with a Kingdom announcement or declaration. The announcement or declaration is that Jesus has all authority and power. The reason why this is extremely important and cannot be overlooked is because as believers in Christ, we are sent with His authority and His power.

> *"For in Christ all the fullness of the Deity lives in bodily form, and in Christ you have been brought to fullness. He is the head over every power and authority."*
>
> **Colossians 2:9-10**

GO

When we go into a place, whether that be a foreign country on a mission trip or just the coffee shop down the street, we carry with us the same command: to tell others about Jesus and to be initiators of God's Kingdom. In other words, we are to live gospel-centered, Kingdom-driven lives. All of us are agents and ambassadors for Jesus to those who are lost and separated from God.

> *"Therefore, we are ambassadors for Christ, God making his appeal through us. We implore you on behalf of Christ, be reconciled to God."*
>
> **2 Corinthians 5:20**

Every follower of Jesus is called to live a gospel-centered, Kingdom-driven life, empowered by the Holy Spirit, to bring God's Kingdom into the life of others. It is our privilege and purpose to participate fully in God's mission to reconcile all people back to Himself. As the people of God's Kingdom, whenever we walk onto the scene, we are bringing His Kingdom into that place. We are declaring, both verbally and non-verbally, who Jesus is and what He has done for people everywhere.

A disciple of Jesus Christ understands that they have been sent by God to bring the gospel of the Kingdom of God to whomever they encounter.

> *"Jesus said to them again, Peace be with you. As the Father has sent me, even so I am sending you."*
>
> **John 20:21**

What are the essentials that people need to know to begin a relationship with Jesus?

First, they need to acknowledge that we are all sinners and we need a Savior.

"For all have sinned and fall short of the glory of God."

Romans 3:23

Second, they need to know that as a result of sin we are all separated from God and spiritually dead.

"For the wages of sin is death, but the gift of God is eternal life in Christ Jesus our Lord."

Romans 6:23

> **The Kingdom commission of Jesus is a vision for discipleship. Discipleship is not a one time event, it is a lifelong journey.**

Third, they need to know that God sent Jesus to die on the cross, paid the penalty for our sin, and brought His Kingdom into our lives.

"But God demonstrates his own love for us in this: While we were still sinners, Christ died for us."

Romans 5:8

Finally, they need to know that to begin a relationship with Jesus we need to receive him into our life as our Savior and King.

> *"Yet to all who received him, to those who believed on his name, he gave the right to become children of God."*
>
> **John 1:12**

As we share these truths with people, along with showing God's love, God will work in their hearts and many will take the first steps to begin a relationship with God. God wants to use us in this supernatural process of bringing the gospel of His Kingdom into the lives of people.

> *"For I am not ashamed of the gospel, because it is the power of God that brings salvation to everyone who believes: first to the Jew, then to the Gentile."*
>
> **Romans 1:16**

MAKE DISCIPLES

The second part of the great commission is to make disciples. While the Bible is clear that we cannot change anyone's heart, we do play a huge role in the process of someone choosing to follow Jesus Christ. A basic definition of discipleship is simply helping someone become a fully devoted follower of Jesus Christ. There are many steps along the way to becoming fully devoted. The following passages give us insight into the life of a disciple.

A Disciple Proclaims the Gospel

> *"For everyone who calls on the name of the Lord will be saved. How then will they call on him in whom they have not believed? And how are they to believe in him of whom they have never heard? And how are they to hear without someone preaching? And how are they to preach unless they are sent? As it is written, How beautiful are the feet of those who preach the good news!"*
>
> **Romans 10:13-15**

A Disciple Encourages Others

"And let us consider how we may spur one another on toward love and good deeds, not giving up meeting together, as some are in the habit of doing, but encouraging one another —and all the more as you see the Day approaching."

Hebrews 10:24-25

A Disciple Engages Truth

"To the Jews who had believed him, Jesus said, "If you hold to my teaching, you are really my disciples. Then you will know the truth, and the truth will set you free."

John 8:31-32

A Disciple Imitates Jesus

"Follow my example, as I follow the example of Christ."

1 Corinthians 11:1

A disciple, or follower of Jesus should reflect in their life the qualities, love and lifestyle of Jesus. We are to live in such unity and harmony with Christ, that it is evident to all who know us. It is God's role to change hearts and our role to direct others toward Him.

Do you know of anyone you can disciple? If so who?

_____

_____

OF ALL NATIONS

Fully devoted followers of Jesus should be involved in taking the gospel to friends, family and neighbors, as well as the rest of the world. There are many places outside of the United States where people have very little opportunity to hear about Jesus and His Kingdom. As followers of Jesus we are to be people who understand that the gospel is not geographically exclusive or limited. God is a global God and His Kingdom is a global Kingdom.

There are several ways that we can participate in sharing the gospel around the world.

Financial Support

We can give a portion of our financial resources to invest in others who are actively bringing the gospel of the Kingdom of God to various countries and people groups.

Prayer

We can pray that God will open hearts and doors in other countries where missionaries are living and sharing the good news of the Kingdom. We may not be physically present, but through our prayers we can trust God is working.

Calling and Trips

We can give, we can pray and we can also go. God may call some of us to become cross-cultural missionaries and move to another country to share the good news of His Kingdom. For the rest of us, we have opportunities to participate on short-term mission trips to assist local missionaries in other countries. As we share God's love with people in other countries God broadens our world-view and we catch a glimpse of how God's Kingdom is growing around the world.

I WILL BE WITH YOU

The Kingdom commission given by Jesus begins with focusing on power and ends by focusing on a promise. The promise of Jesus is that no matter where you go and what you do, He will be with you. He promises His presence as the source of comfort, security, and peace needed along the journey. This is the great promise, from the King of Kings, to His people.

What does the great commission teach us as a follower of Jesus?

_____

_____

Describe the difference between the kingdom commandment and the kingdom commission.

_____

_____

_____

_____

LOOKING AT WHAT YOU LEARNED

Fill in the blanks below:

The command Jesus gave us is an _____, _____, and _____ command.

It is only out of our love for _____ that we are able to love _____ and _____.

All of us are _____ of Jesus Christ to those who do not know Jesus.

Discipleship is simply helping someone become a _____-_____ follower of Jesus Christ.

Our role is to _____ others about Jesus; God's role is to _____ their heart.

How has this chapter contributed toward your understanding of God and His desire for your life?

What did this chapter teach you about the command and commission of Jesus?

Did you have any questions after reading this chapter?

RECOMMENDED FURTHER RESOURCES

Not a Fan by Kyle Idleman

Walk Across the Room by Bill Hybels

Discipleship by Dietrich Bonhoeffer

Discipleship Essentials by Greg Oden

Gospel-Centered Discipleship by Jonathan Dodson

Let the Nations Be Glad by John Piper

Becoming a Contagious Christian by Bill Hybles

The Purpose Driven Life by Rick Warren

Gospel Commission by Michael Horton

The Jesus Creed by Scot McKnight

MY ASSIGNMENT FOR THIS WEEK IS:

NOTES

NOTES

PART 7:
DISCIPLINES &
DISCERNMENT
IN THE KINGDOM

PART 7: DISCIPLINES & DISCERNMENT

As we end our journey exploring what it is like to live life as a disciple for the King and in His Kingdom, we will finish by looking at three significant spiritual disciplines. We will also look at a helpful approach to spiritual discernment.

SPIRITUAL DISCIPLINES

Spiritual disciplines are specific practices that we put in place to allow us to orient and center our life on God's Kingdom agenda and purposes. We have already talked about the spiritual discipline of learning about God through the Bible and communicating with God in prayer. These are two of the most important disciplines we can engage in on a regular basis, but there are also others that are extremely helpful and formative. It is out of a desire to delight in God and His Kingdom that we engage in spiritual disciplines.

What is a spiritual discipline?

_____

_____

The three specific spiritual disciplines we will walk through in this chapter are rest, financial stewardship, and worship.

SPIRITUAL DISCIPLINE OF REST

We live in a fast-paced world and often feel the pressure of falling behind and being overwhelmed. However, in the chaos of life as a follower of Jesus, we are called to rest. A person's ability to rest is one of the greatest indicators of their emotional and spiritual health. The practice of taking time to rest might be the most neglected, yet most needed spiritual discipline in our life.

Barbara Brown Taylor in her book *Divine Subtraction* put it best, "Some of us have made an idol of exhaustion. The only time we know we have done enough is when we are running on empty and when the ones we love most are the ones we see the least. When we lie down to sleep at night, we offer our full appointment calendars to God in lieu of prayer, believing that God – who is as busy as we are – will surely understand."

When we come to the Bible, we find that God places a very high priority on rest. The word for rest in the Bible is the word Sabbath. The word Sabbath means to "cease" or to "stop." In the Old Testament, the people of God devoted an entire day to rest as an aspect of their obedience and worship. In the New Testament, Jesus becomes our place of rest, but we still are to be people who take rest seriously. The spiritual discipline of rest allows us to enjoy God, enjoy others, and trust God.

"Remember the Sabbath day by keeping it holy."
Exodus 20:8

"If you keep your feet from breaking the Sabbath and from doing as you please on my holy day, if you call the Sabbath a delight and the Lord's holy day honorable, and if you honor it by not going your own way and not doing as you please or speaking idle words, then you will find your joy in the Lord."

Isaiah 58:13-14a

"Come to me, all you who are weary and burdened, and I will give you rest. Take my yoke upon you and learn from me, for I am gentle and humble in heart, and you will find rest for your souls. For my yoke is easy and my burden is light."

Matthew 11:28-30

What is the spiritual discipline of rest?

_____

_____

_____

_____

It is out of a desire to delight in God and His Kingdom that we engage in spiritual disciplines.

It is with this in mind that we suggest setting aside one day a week devoted to rest. Every person is different and therefore what works for you, may not work for another person. The most important thing is that you make an intentional effort to rest. When organizing a day devoted to rest consider the following structure as a guide.

REST

Take time to get plenty of sleep. Consider turning the alarm clock off and unplugging from anything that involves your typical everyday work life. It might be worth considering not checking e-mails, not checking Facebook, turning off your phone and even taking a nap.

REFLECT

Reflect on the character of God and the gifts He has given to you. It might be worth considering reading larger portions of God's Word and carving out extra time just to thank God for the various blessings in your life.

RECREATION

Take time to do things that replenish you. Sometimes we forget to laugh and have fun. It is worth considering what activities give you life and then plan on participating in them. If it is running, go for a run. If it is playing basketball, go play basketball. If it is gardening, enjoy some time in the garden. In recreation, we are re-created.

REMEMBER

Remember the goodness and grace of God. In your time of prayer remember that you were saved by God's grace to live in His Kingdom and be about His Kingdom work. Remember the gospel and reflect on what it means to be a disciple who is in Christ.

SPIRITUAL DISCIPLINE OF FINANCIAL STEWARDSHIP

God has entrusted certain resources to us such as time, spiritual gifts, relationships, and finances. We have the privilege and responsibility of managing or stewarding those resources. The spiritual discipline of financial stewardship is all about managing our finances in a way that honors God and extends His Kingdom. The way we steward our finances ultimately reveals the condition of our heart.

"Do not store up for yourselves treasures on earth, where moths and vermin destroy, and where thieves break in and steal. But store up for yourselves treasures in heaven, where moths and

vermin do not destroy, and where thieves do not break in and steal. For where your treasure is, there your heart will be also."

Matthew 6:19-21

What is the spiritual discipline of stewardship?

_____

_____

Financial stewardship reveals our heart and directs us toward God's agenda and priorities. How does someone steward the finances God has entrusted to him or her? Below is a list of some helpful guidelines to follow as you exercise the spiritual discipline of stewardship.

IDENTIFY YOUR FINANCIAL ENEMIES

We all have specific areas in our life that keep us from financial freedom. If we are going to steward the resources God has entrusted to us, we must identify our enemies. The primary enemy of our financial stewardship is debt. Debt happens whenever we owe something to another. Although it is not exclusively forbidden in the Bible, it is certainly discouraged.

"Let no debt remain outstanding, except the continuing debt to love one another..."

Romans 13:8a

"The rich rule over the poor, and the borrower is slave to the lender."

Proverbs 22:7

UNDERSTANDING YOUR FINANCIAL BLESSINGS

God entrusts us with finances, so that we can save, spend, and give generously. We are blessed by God to be a blessing to others. All of our resources are a gift from God. When we understand this truth, it changes us from the inside out. We no longer look at finances as a burden, but instead as a blessing.

"You may say to yourself, "My power and the strength of my hands have produced this wealth for me." But remember the LORD your God, for it is He who gives you the ability to produce wealth, and so confirms His covenant, which he swore to your forefathers, as it is today."

Deuteronomy 8:17-18

"Honor the LORD with your wealth, with the firstfruits of all your crops; then your barns will be filled to overflowing, and your vats will brim over with new wine."

Proverbs 3:9-10

HONORING GOD THROUGH GIVING

Honoring God with our resources is an important part of life in God's Kingdom. We could give our finances to any multitude of ministries that exist, but a primary place for giving should be our local church. In the Bible when people give their finances as an aspect of worshiping God it fits into two categories. The categories are tithes and offerings.

"Return to me, and I will return to you," says the Lord Almighty. "But you ask, 'How are we to return?' "Will a mere mortal rob God? Yet you rob me. "But you ask, 'How are we robbing you?' "In tithes and offerings. You are under a curse —your whole nation—because you are robbing me. Bring the whole tithe into the storehouse, that there may be food in my house. Test me in this," says the Lord Almighty, "and see if I will not throw open the floodgates of heaven and pour out so much blessing that there will not be room enough to store it."

Malachi 3:7b-10

In the Old Testament, the people of God were required to regularly give a "tithe" (meaning tenth) of their overall income to God. They also made additional contributions during other parts of the year. Any additional contributions were considered to be an offering. An offering is anything above and beyond a tithe. This same concept has carried over into the life of the church. The most important thing is that a person is stewarding the financial resources that God has entrusted to them in a way that honors God and extends His Kingdom.

What is the difference between a tithe and an offering?

_____

_____

SPIRITUAL DISCIPLINE OF WORSHIP

According to the dictionary, worship means to honor and regard with extravagant reverence or devotion. The spiritual discipline of worship is the discipline of honoring God, praising God, celebrating God, and revering God despite present circumstances or specific seasons of life. We worship God because He is worthy of our worship. When we worship God we are ultimately bringing glory to His name.

> "Ascribe to the Lord the glory due His name; worship the Lord in the splendor of His holiness."
>
> **Psalm 29:2**

> "You are worthy, our Lord and God, to receive glory and honor and power, for you created all things, and by your will they were created and have their being."
>
> **Revelation 4:11**

What is the spiritual discipline of worship?

_____

_____

Worshiping anything other than God is idolatry. Idolatry is taking a good thing and making it a God thing. When we worship anything smaller than Jesus for our salvation, sense of security, identity, and primary source of fulfillment we are committing idolatry. Idolatry happens inside the church and outside the church. We must constantly guard ourselves from idolatry and continually engage in God honoring, God glorifying worship.

One of the ways we can worship God is through singing songs either in private or in public services. Worship is certainly not limited to singing songs, but songs are a key way we are invited into worshiping God. It is with this in mind that we suggest some practices that will help you engage even further in worship through song.

> *"Let the message of Christ dwell among you richly as you teach and admonish one another with all wisdom through psalms, hymns, and songs from the Spirit, singing to God with gratitude in your hearts."*
>
> **Colossians 3:16**

PREPARE YOUR HEART

On Sunday mornings before engaging in worship through song, take a moment to prepare your heart. The easiest way to do this is on your drive over to church. Instead of listening to the radio, take a moment to pray. In your time of prayer confess your sin, thank God for His grace and ask for His empowering presence in your time of worship.

> *"Guard your steps when you go to the house of God."*
>
> **Ecclesiastes 5:1a**

CLOSE YOUR EYES

God has given us built in blindfolds to help us concentrate and not be distracted. As you worship God, learn to memorize the words and then with eyes closed, sing your heart out. When our eyes are opened it is easy to pay attention to what is going on around us instead of what is going on in us.

LIFT YOUR HANDS

When your arms are raised and your hands are open it is a sign of both receiving and giving. Raising your hands allows you to express to God the posture of your heart with your body. At first it might be uncomfortable, but it will soon lead toward freedom and joy.

Remember that the most important response in worship is one that is authentic and sincere. The Bible mentions different postures and practices in worship: kneeling, standing, lifting hands, shouts of praise and singing, just to mention a few. Express your worship to God with freedom, passion, and joy.

"I will praise you as long as I live, and in your name I will lift up my hands."

Psalm 63:4

SPIRITUAL DISCERNMENT

It is one thing to practice spiritual disciplines and another thing to feel comfortable practicing spiritual discernment.

> **Spiritual discernment is the ability to recognize God's leading and direction in a given situation or circumstance.**

Spiritual discernment is the ability to recognize God's leading and direction in a given situation or circumstance. In order to participate in healthy spiritual discernment we have to understand the multi-faceted concept of God's will. When learning about God's will we can refer to His general will or specific will.

What is spiritual discernment?

_____

_____

GENERAL WILL

God has a general will for our life that isn't hidden or vague. His general will falls into two main categories. They are as follows:

SOVEREIGN PLAN

God is ultimately in control and has a plan for the future that cannot be trumped or derailed by anyone or anything. We can't fully understand or comprehend His sovereign plan, but that doesn't mean He doesn't have one. We must trust that He is in control.

> "And we know that in all things God works for the good of those who love him, who have been called according to His purpose."
>
> **Romans 8:28**

> "Oh, the depth of the riches of the wisdom and knowledge of God! How unsearchable his judgments, and his paths beyond tracing out!"
>
> **Romans 11:33**

REVEALED PLAN

God has already revealed to us His intentions and desires for the majority of our life through His Word. We do not need to wrestle in prayer over these as much as respond in obedience. Below are two examples of God's revealed plan for our lives.

Repent and Receive Jesus as Savior and King

> "The Lord is not slow in keeping His promise, as some understand slowness. Instead he is patient with you, not wanting anyone to perish, but everyone to come to repentance."
>
> **2 Peter 3:9**

Live like Jesus

"Whoever claims to live in Him must live as Jesus did."

1 John 2:6

SPECIFIC WILL

God does not just have a general will for our life, He also has a specific will for our life. He has specific things that He is calling us to do that are a part of His redemptive work in history. It is far easier to rest in God's general will than to discover His specific will for our life. Discovering God's specific will can be both exciting and overwhelming. It is far more of a lifelong journey than a determined destination.

"For we are God's handiwork, created in Christ Jesus to do good works, which God prepared in advance for us to do."

Ephesians 2:10

In order to discover God's specific will, we must keep in mind that God is not sadistic or manipulative. Discovering God's specific will is far more about guidance than it is about guessing. In our journey, God graciously gives us resources to help us process and discern as we strive to make wise and at times difficult decisions. Below are some resources we should lean into to help us discern what might be God's specific will for our life.

THE BIBLE

The more we come to know God's Word the more we are able to discern the difference between God's general will and God's specific will. We use God's Word as a guide for all our decisions.

"Your word is a lamp for my feet, a light on my path."

Psalm 119:105

PRAYER

Prayer is not just talking to God, but also listening to God. Many times, God will prompt us through prayer to have greater understanding of His specific will.

"The prayer of a righteous person is powerful and effective."
James 5:16b

HOLY SPIRIT

The Holy Spirit empowers us. In many ways, the Holy Spirit is our secret weapon. He is the inside source that enables us to experience more of God's rule and reign in our life. The promptings we receive through prayer are from the Holy Spirit unless they contradict the clear teaching of the Bible.

"And I will ask the Father, and he will give you another advocate to help you and be with you forever— the Spirit of truth. The world cannot accept Him, because it neither sees Him nor knows Him. But you know Him, for he lives with you and will be in you."
John 14:16-17

PEOPLE OF GOD

Many times we struggle with perspective and a desire for affirmation or correction. God puts people in our life for a reason. A healthy aspect of spiritual discernment is taking time to tap into the wisdom that comes from seeking counsel from mature and trusted believers.

"Plans fail for lack of counsel, but with many advisers they succeed."
Proverbs 15:22

What is the difference between God's general will and God's specific will?

_____

_____

LOOKING AT WHAT YOU LEARNED

Fill in the blanks below:

Spiritual disciplines help us focus on God's Kingdom
_____.

The word used for rest in the Bible is the word
_____.

Stewardship is managing what God has _____
to us.

The opposite of worship is _____.

God has a _____ will and
_____ will for our life.

TAKING TIME TO REFLECT FURTHER

How has this chapter contributed toward your understanding of God and His desire for your life?

How did this help you better understand spiritual disciplines and spiritual discernment?

Did you have any questions after reading this chapter?

RECOMMENDED FURTHER RESOURCES

Celebration of Disciplines by Richard Foster

Experiencing God by Henry Blackaby

Total Money Makeover by Dave Ramsey

The Treasure Principle by Randy Alcorn

The Life You've Always Wanted by John Ortberg

Leading on Empty by Wayne Cordeiro

Spiritual Disciplines for the Christian Life by Donald Whitney

The Purpose of Man by A.W. Tozer

The Air I Breathe by Louie Giglo

The Rest of God by Mark Buchanan

The Discipline of Spiritual Discernment by Tim Challies

MY ASSIGNMENT FOR THIS WEEK IS:

NOTES

NOTES

FINAL WORDS OF ENCOURAGEMENT

You made it! It is important to celebrate the journey you have taken over the past seven weeks, which we trust has been a source of encouragement, empowerment, and education. **It is our hope that you will devote your life to making disciples.** Just as you were discipled, God wants you to disciple others.

As you continue forward growing in your relationship with God, may you never forget the grace and love of God. You are called by the King to be about His redemptive purposes. It is a joy and privilege, a responsibility and an opportunity to bring glory to His name and extend His Kingdom. Enjoy the process and intentionally center your life to see His Kingdom come!

"Being confident of this, that he who began a good work in you will carry it on to completion until the day of Christ Jesus."
Philippians 1:6

GLOSSARY OF HELPFUL BIBLICAL TERMS

Adoption: The supernatural work of God to bring a person into His family. Adoption takes place through receiving Jesus Christ and entering into God's Kingdom.

Atonement : The decisive act of God to deal with the human problem of sin by sending His Son as a complete sacrifice to reconcile us to God. This reconciliation took place on the cross and through the resurrection.

Baptism: The outward public declaration and profession of putting your faith in Jesus Christ. It is not a requirement for salvation, but it is the next step after salvation. The word baptism means immersion.

Christ: The English translation of the Greek word meaning messiah or anointed one. Christ is a title, not a name. It refers to someone who will deliver God's people and set up His Kingdom.

Church: A group of people who make up the family of God. In the Old Testament the people of God were called the Israelites. In the New Testament the people of God are referred to as the church. The word church means, a called out gathering. The local church is a representation of the global church.

Communion or Eucharist: The intentional time that believers gather to remember and reflect on the life and death of Jesus. It is a time to give thanks for His sacrifice for us. The word Eucharist means thanksgiving.

Conversion: What happens when a person turns from their sins and trust in Jesus as their Savior. They are no longer dead to sin, but have been made alive in Christ. They are no longer outside the Kingdom of God; they are now inside the Kingdom of God.

Denomination: Several congregations or local churches that unite together around a common belief and vision.

Doctrine: A person's teaching or beliefs.

Glorification: The last stage in the process or order of salvation and refers to the second coming of Jesus when a person will receive a resurrection body.

Grace: One of the central concepts in scripture. There are various forms of grace in scripture ranging from God's common grace to His saving grace. The term refers to a gift of God that is not based on anything a person does to earn that gift. Grace is God's riches at Christ's expense. It is an unconditional gift, given to an undeserving person, by and unobligated giver.

Heaven and Hell: Heaven refers to the place of God's presence, while the term Hell refers to the absence of God's presence. Both of these are literal, eternal and eventual destinations. A person will either spend eternity with God or an eternity without God. An eternity with God is what scripture writers refer to as heaven and an eternity without God is what scripture writers refer to as hell.

Holy: Set apart or sacred.

Immutability: The consistency of God's character. God is unchanging and faithful, when it comes to His character.

Incarnation: The ability of Jesus to be both God and man while here on earth. It refers to Jesus taking on humanity, while still keeping His divinity.

Inerrancy: The faithfulness and accuracy of the Bible when it comes to substance and teaching. If something is inerrant it is without error.

Inspiration: The process of God's supernatural work to bring about the Bible through human authors.

Justification: The divine act whereby God makes those who are sinful, fully acceptable before a holy God. It is a legal declaration of a new identity, nature, family, and future. It takes place by grace and grace alone.

Kingdom of God: The rule and reign of God, the power and presence of God, made available and accessible through the person and work of Jesus.

Law: God's revealed rules and regulations in the Old Testament that were put in place to lead people into a deeper restored relationship with God. In the New Testament, Jesus does not abolish the law, but fulfills it. Jesus becomes the standard by which a person can have a restored relationship with God. The law was never meant to bring about salvation, but rather to point people to a God that saves.

Redemption: The process by which sinful people are brought back from their bondage of sin and brought into God's family. It is a metaphorical picture in the Bible of God's grace in action.

Righteousness: God's just character or a person's right standing before a Holy God. Righteousness is given to a believer through justification as part of God's work in salvation.

Salvation: The overall process a person goes through to enter into God's Kingdom. Salvation is God's rescue of humanity from the consequences of sin and into a personal relationship with Jesus Christ and His Kingdom, for both now and all eternity.

Sanctification: The process of being set apart or made holy. It is the ongoing partnership between God and man after salvation for the purpose of spiritual growth and maturity. It is initiated and superintendent by God.

Sin: An inherited spiritual condition and a direct choice to not live under the rule and reign of God. People are born into this world with a sinful condition. This condition separates us from a holy and just God. When we enter into God's Kingdom through salvation the penalty of sin is removed from our life. Sin is not just a spiritual condition, but it is also a choice. Whenever a person chooses to live life apart from God's rule and reign they choose to sin. A person can be a follower of Jesus and still sin. The penalty of sin may be removed, but the power and presence of sin is still very real and tangible.

Sovereign: God's kingly supreme rule and reign. God is sovereign, meaning He is in control and on the throne.

Theology: The study of God, His work, and His ways.

Trinity: The biblical understanding of God as three, but one. God is triune and yet one. They are equal in personhood, but different in revealed roles.

Wrath of God: The free, subjective, and holy response of God to sin, evil, and wickedness by those in opposition to God.

LEADERS
GUIDE
IN THE KINGDOM

DISCIPLER'S LEADERS GUIDE

WELCOME TO THE JOURNEY

We want to welcome you into this discipleship journey of helping another person move forward in becoming a fully devoted follower of Jesus. We believe being involved in a discipleship relationship is truly a joy, privilege, and responsibility. It is our hope that through this discipleship leaders guide you will feel empowered and encouraged to successfully lead others toward a deeper experience of God's Kingdom in their life.

BEST PRACTICES

In order to get the most out of each and every session, we encourage and expect you to follow a list of best practices described in the details below.

PREPARATION

Almost everyone has been a part of some situation where it was obvious that the person leading was not prepared to lead. They fumble over their words, they don't know what is happening next and as a result you can't wait for it all to be over. In many ways, the success or failure of this discipleship relationship will come down to your level of preparation. When a leader is prepared those they are leading feel cared for and respected.

PREPARE YOUR HEART

Make time before you meet with the person you are discipling and prepare your heart. It is not enough to know the information. You need to be focused on transformation. Before asking God to work in another person's heart, we need to start by asking Him to work in our heart.

PREPARE YOUR MIND

Make time not only to prepare your heart, but also to prepare your mind. Read over the session ahead of time, look through the leader's guide and have a solid sense of direction before you meet with the person you are discipling.

PLANNING

As a discipler you have a limited amount of time to make a lasting impact. Therefore, it is vital to make the most of your time with the person you are discipling. You want to be smart and strategic as you think through what you will be covering and discussing.

PICKING THE RIGHT PLACE AND TIME

Where you meet and when you meet are very important decisions. We recommend you choose a safe place that has limited distractions and choose a time that is beneficial for both of you.

THE STRUCTURE OF A MEETING

Now that you are prepared and have a set place and time, the next step is to layout what you will be doing when you meet together. Here is a suggested breakdown of how to spend an hour together.

Beginning Point - 15 Minutes

Take the first fifteen minutes to get to know each other and get a sense for the others persons week. Ask simple questions like, "How was your week" or "How was your day?" End the beginning point with taking time to pray before going further.

Developing Point - 30 Minutes

After taking a moment to pray, a great way to capitalize on your time together is to read each passage in that chapter out loud. Over the next thirty minutes, use the leader's guide to walk back through the previous session. Take your time and make sure they really understand what they just read and processed. Ask questions, clarify answers and listen more than you talk.

Tipping Point - 15 Minutes

Take the last fifteen minutes to focus less on the information and more on the person's heart. Help them connect the dots and see how this makes a difference in their spiritual life. End the time by giving assignments for next week and praying for each other.

GUIDING AND FACILITATING

As a discipler your main role is to guide and facilitate with the heart of a teacher. We cannot change people, but we can encourage and direct them to a God who can bring change in their life.

LISTEN AND ASK QUESTIONS

One of the worst things a discipler can do is to talk the whole time. You may be thinking in your mind right now, "but I have so many great things to say." I am sure you do, but saying them at the right time and in the right way is just as important as saying them. A great discipler is a facilitator over an educator. A general rule to follow is what is called the 60/40 rule. The discipler talks 40 percent of the time and facilitates with questions, so the person being discipled talks 60 percent of the time.

VULNERABILITY, TRANSPARENCY, AND HONESTY

A discipler who is vulnerable is both transparent and honest with the person they are discipling. If you do not know the answer don't pretend that you do. When the opportunity arises you can share details about your journey, setbacks and points of celebration.

ENCOURAGEMENT, AFFIRMATION, AND CHALLENGE

One of the great opportunities as a guide and facilitator is to encourage, affirm and challenge the person you are discipling. At certain points you will discover more about their life and as you do, listen well, so that you can in turn lead well.

PART 1:
THE KINGDOM STORY
THE KING & HIS KINGDOM

PART 1: THE KINGDOM STORY

QUICK SUMMARY

The goal of this chapter is to help the person being discipled learn the story of the Kingdom of God. They should be able to understand the big picture of scripture as well as define the following terms: disciple, Kingdom of God, gospel, Jesus Christ, etc.

PRAY THE KINGDOM PRAYER

Father in Heaven your Kingdom come in me and through me today. Amen!

STARTING POINT

In the very beginning take some time to share with each other a little more about the following: Where did you grow up? What do you do for a living? What are your hobbies? The most important decision you make in the beginning is to spend plenty of time getting to know the person you are discipling. Take your time! Afterwards, make the point that it is helpful to know about each other's story. It is out of knowing the story that you are able to build more and more trust. The same is true when it comes to God's story in human history. When we understand the story of the Kingdom of God it sets the foundation for more and more trust.

Take a moment to read out loud together all of the passages in this section.

FILL IN THE BLANKS

Below are the fill in the blanks for this chapter. Take a moment in the Developing Point to make sure they have these successfully filled out.

What is a disciple?

A disciple is a devoted follower of Jesus.

What is the Kingdom of God?

The Kingdom of God is the power and presence, rule and reign of God made available and accessible to us in and through Jesus.

What does the name Jesus Christ mean?

Savior King.

What does the word gospel mean?

Good news.

What does it mean that the Kingdom of God has come, but not yet fully?

One day Jesus is coming back to fully set up His Kingdom. The first time He came the Kingdom started, but the second time He comes the Kingdom will be fully set up and established.

The Kingdom of God came first in the <u>GARDEN OF EDEN</u>.

The Kingdom of God then came through <u>THE PROMISE</u> given to Abraham.

The Kingdom of God was in the <u>TENT OF MEETINGS</u> in the wilderness.

The Kingdom of God was in the <u>TEMPLE</u> built by Solomon.

The Kingdom of God was prophesied about by the <u>PROPHETS</u>.

The Kingdom of God finally came through the King of Kings <u>JESUS CHRIST</u> in the New Testament.

The Kingdom will fully come when Jesus comes back the <u>SECOND</u> time.

GOING DEEPER

The following is a list of questions from the acronym L.E.A.D that gives you a better picture into how this chapter shaped their understanding of what it means to follow Jesus.

L - LEARNING

What did you learn about the Kingdom of God?

What did you learn about Jesus as the King?

What questions did you have after reading this chapter?

E - ENCOURAGED

How does understanding the story of the Kingdom of God encourage you as a follower of Jesus?

A - APPLYING

How does understanding the big picture of what God has been doing, and is doing, help you in your journey forward with Him?

D - DIRECT TO PRAYER

How can I pray for you this week, especially as it relates to the Kingdom of God?

EXTRA QUESTIONS

Below is room for you to write down extra questions that you want to ask in your time together.

ASSIGNMENT FOR NEXT WEEK

Each week give the person you are discipling an assignment for the next week. Have them write it down in the notes section of their guide.

On one sheet of paper write down how you came into a relationship with Jesus. You can break this up into three sections: your life before Jesus, when you started a relationship with Jesus and your life after starting a relationship with Jesus.

NOTES

PART 2:
SALVATION
IN THE KINGDOM

PART 2: SALVATION

QUICK SUMMARY

The goal of this chapter is to help the person being discipled learn about the subject of salvation. They should be able to understand what they are saved from, and what they are saved too, as well as define the following terms: sin, sacrifice, adoption, justification, etc.

PRAY THE KINGDOM PRAYER

Father in Heaven your Kingdom come in me and through me today. Amen!

STARTING POINT

In the very beginning, take some time to listen to their salvation story. Remember this was their assignment for last week. Make sure to ask plenty of questions about their salvation experience, then take time to share your story. When you share you story of faith, be specific, detailed, and don't rush. This is an important time together.

Take a moment to read out loud together all of the passages in this section.

FILL IN THE BLANKS

Below are the fill in the blanks for this chapter. Take a moment in the Developing Point to make sure they have these successfully filled out.

What is sin and what does it accomplish in our life?

Sin is both a condition and a choice. It leads to separation from God and death. As a believer, we are confident before Jesus that our salvation is not in question when we sin, but our fellowship with God is damaged and broken.

What did God do to resolve our sin problem?

God sent His Son to be a complete sacrifice for our sin. When we put our faith in Jesus, we are receiving His work on the cross for our sin. He paid the penalty of sin, so that we could freely receive eternal life.

Why is it important to have a correct understanding of Jesus?

If we reduce Jesus to anything other than the Son of God we miss the seriousness of sin and the reality of the Savior. Jesus is not just a teacher or a prophet. Jesus is the Son of God.

What are some things that people do to try and make themselves right with God?

Read more scriptures, serve a ministry or non-profit, try to live without sin, emotionally beat themselves up, etc.

Is sin completely removed from our life after we experience salvation?

No. The penalty of sin is removed. We are no longer separated from God, but securely adopted into His family. The power of sin is still very real. After becoming a believer, sin can ruin your marriage, work life, fellowship with God, etc.

What is the process of salvation?

Regeneration, Conversion, Justification, Sanctification, and Glorification.

Salvation is God's RESCUE of humanity from the CONSEQUENCES of sin and into a PERSONAL relationship with Himself for both NOW and ETERNITY.

Salvation cannot be EARNED. It can only be RECEIVED.

We are saved from our SIN and into ADOPTION as a member of God's family.

We are saved from the PENALTY of sin, but sin still has POWER in our lives.

The process of salvation is as follows: REGENERATION, CONVERSION, JUSTIFICATION, SANCTIFICATION, and GLORIFICATION.

GOING DEEPER

The following is a list of questions from the acronym L.E.A.D that gives you a better picture into how this chapter shaped their understanding of what it means to follow Jesus.

L - LEARNING

What did you learn about the subject of salvation?

What did you learn about the forgiveness of sin and adoption in the family of God?

What questions did you have after reading this chapter?

E - ENCOURAGED

How does understanding the subject of salvation encourage you as a follower of Jesus?

A - APPLYING

How does understanding the subject of salvation help you in your journey forward with Him?

D - DIRECT TO PRAYER

How can I pray for you this week, especially as it relates to the subject of salvation?

EXTRA QUESTIONS

Below is room for you to write down extra questions that you want to ask in your time together.

ASSIGNMENT FOR NEXT WEEK

Each week give the person you are discipling an assignment for next week. Have them write it down in the notes section of their guide.

Ask them to prayerfully consider sharing their story of faith with someone else. Some of the ways they can do this is as follows: Posting their salvation story on facebook, sitting down with family, friends or a co-worker, or even signing up to share their salvation story with a ministry of the church.

Share with them that next week you will be talking about spending time in scripture as part of your life as a follower of Jesus. Ask them to write down what is their favorite book of the Bible and why? Do they have a plan to read scripture and if so, what does it look like? Have them download the YouVersion app for their phone as a great resource for engaging scripture.

NOTES

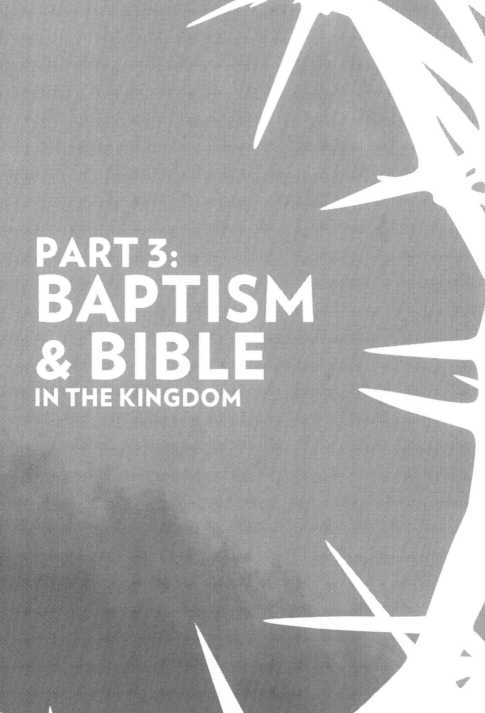

PART 3:
BAPTISM
& BIBLE
IN THE KINGDOM

PART 3: BAPTISM & BIBLE

QUICK SUMMARY

The goal of this chapter is to help the person being discipled learn about the subject of baptism as well as gain more confidence reading the Bible. They should be able to understand the following terms: baptism, Bible, inspiration of scripture, etc.

PRAY THE KINGDOM PRAYER

Father in Heaven your Kingdom come in me and through me today. Amen!

STARTING POINT

In the very beginning take some time to find out if that person has a favorite book or letter of the Bible. Find out what version they are reading and the answer to the questions you asked last week. Share your favorite book of the Bible, what version you read and the importance of God's Word in our life. Share with them that the Bible informs our understanding of life in the Kingdom, especially the subject of Baptism. Go from there.

Take a moment to read out loud together all of the passages in this section.

FILL IN THE BLANKS

Below are the fill in the blanks for this chapter. Take a moment in the Developing Point to make sure they have these successfully filled out.

Define in one sentence the practice of baptism?

The declaration of Jesus as King through immersion in water.

What did you learn about the life and teachings of Jesus as it relates to baptism?

Let them share their answer to this question.

What is the difference between baptism and baby dedication?

Baptism is an outward declaration that a person is a follower of Jesus. Baby dedication is a parental commitment to raise a child in a way that honors and glorifies God.

How many times does someone need to get baptized?

Once.

Why should a follower of Jesus get baptized?

They should get baptized as an act of obedience and commitment to Jesus.

What do we learn from the Bible?

We learn about the character of God, the Kingdom of God, and the life we are called to live as followers of Jesus.

What makes the Bible different from any other book?

It is inspired by God and everything in the Bible points to the person of Jesus and His Kingdom.

What do the words Bible and testament mean?

Bible means book or books and the word testament means covenant or contract. Neither term is actually used in scripture.

How many books are in the Old Testament and what is the structure?

39 books in the Old Testament. The structure is as follows: Five books of Moses, Twelve books of History, Five books of Poetry, Seventeen books of the Prophets.

How many books are in the New Testament and what is the structure?

27 books in the Old Testament. The structure is as follows: Gospels, Book of Acts, Epistles or Letters, and Book of Revelation.

What is the difference between observation, interpretation, and application?

In observation you are asking the question, "What do I see?" In interpretation you are asking the question, "What does this mean?" In application you are asking the question, "Now what, so what?"

The word baptism means IMMERSION.

Baptism is not a MEANS for salvation.

Baptism is a public DECLARATION of the INWARD transformation that has taken place in our life through Jesus.

The word Bible means BOOK. The word testament means COVENANT.

The Old Testament was written in HEBREW and the New Testament was primarily written in GREEK.

GOING DEEPER

The following is a list of questions from the acronym L.E.A.D that givesyou a better picture into how this chapter shaped their understanding of what it means to follow Jesus.

L - LEARNING

What did you learn about the subject of baptism?

What did you learn about the importance of the Bible and the structure of the Bible?

Find out if the person has been baptized, and if not, encourage them to be baptized.

What questions did you have after reading this chapter?

E - ENCOURAGED

How does understanding the subject of baptism and the Bible encourage you as a follower of Jesus?

A - APPLYING

How does understanding the subject of baptism and the Bible help you in your journey forward with Him?

D - DIRECT TO PRAYER

How can I pray for you this week, especially as it relates to the subject of engaging in scripture?

EXTRA QUESTIONS

Below is room for you to write down extra questions that you want to ask in your time together.

ASSIGNMENT FOR NEXT WEEK

Each week give the person you are discipling an assignment for next week. Have them write it down in the notes section of their guide.

If they have not yet been baptized, ask them if they are ready and willing to sign up to be baptized. If so, direct them to the right person and place. Celebrate with them the decision to be baptized. Make sure to communicate that you will be there for them as they take this next step in their discipleship journey..

NOTES

PART 4:
PRAYER & COMMUNITY
IN THE KINGDOM

PART 4:
PRAYER &
COMMUNITY

QUICK SUMMARY

The goal of this chapter is to help the person being discipled learn about the subjects of prayer and community. They should be able to understand the following terms: prayer, character of God, community, church, etc.

PRAY THE KINGDOM PRAYER

Father in Heaven your Kingdom come in me and through me today. Amen!

STARTING POINT

In the very beginning take some time to find out about that person's previous church experience. Ask them if they are currently in a life group and if so how has being in a community shaped their spiritual maturity. Take some time to share you experiences as well and then move into this chapter.

Take a moment to read out loud together all of the passages in this section.

FILL IN THE BLANKS

Below are the fill in the blanks for this chapter. Take a moment in the Developing Point to make sure they have these successfully filled out.

What is prayer?

Prayer is communicating with God.

What are the characteristics or attributes of God mentioned?

Omnipotence, Omniscience, Omnipresence, Love and Holiness

What are the two characteristics of a healthy prayer life?

Honesty and Sincerity.

What part of the Lord's Prayer is most difficult and easy for you to pray?

Learn from them and share from your experience.

What is the church?

The church is the New Testament term for the people of God. It means called out ones.

Why is living in community with others so important?

We are designed to live in community and when we do, we are encouraged, supported, and challenged to grow in our relationship with Jesus.

Prayer is <u>COMMUNICATING OR TALKING</u> to God.

When we pray, we should pray with <u>HONESTY</u> and <u>SINCERITY</u>.

Jesus gave us an example of what to pray and how to pray in the

<u>LORD'S PRAYER.</u>

We are created by God and created to live in <u>COMMUNITY</u> with other people.

The word church means <u>CALLED OUT ONES</u>.

GOING DEEPER

The following is a list of question from the acronym L.E.A.D that gives you a better picture into how this chapter shaped their understanding of what it means to follow Jesus.

L - LEARNING

What did you learn about the character or attributes of God?

What did you learn about the subject of prayer?

What did you learn about the importance of community?

What questions did you have after reading this chapter?

E - ENCOURAGED

How does understanding the subject of prayer and community encourage you as a follower of Jesus?

A - APPLYING

How does understanding the subject of prayer and community help you in your journey forward with Him?

D - DIRECT TO PRAYER

How can I pray for you this week, especially as it relates to the subject of prayer and community?

EXTRA QUESTIONS

Below is room for you to write down extra questions that you want to ask in your time together.

ASSIGNMENT FOR NEXT WEEK

Each week give the person you are discipling an assignment for next week. Have them write it down in the notes section of their guide. If they are not in a life group, ask them to consider signing up and taking the step into deeper community. Also ask them if they have ever taken time to discover what might be their spiritual gifts.

If they have not, give them the assignment this week to spend time learning and discovering their spiritual gifts.

NOTES

PART 5:
GROWTH
& POWER
IN THE KINGDOM

PART 5: GROWTH & POWER

QUICK SUMMARY

The goal of this chapter is to help the person being discipled learn about the subject of growth in God's Kingdom and the power available through the Holy Spirit. They should be able to understand how God's Kingdom is dynamic and growing in their life and learn about the person and work of the Holy Spirit. They should be able to understand the following terms: Holy Spirit, Spiritual Gifts, Kingdom Growth, etc.

PRAY THE KINGDOM PRAYER

Father in Heaven your Kingdom come in me and through me today. Amen!

STARTING POINT

As you begin take a moment to talk further about the concept of spiritual gifts. After you finish talking about spiritual gifts talk about spiritual growth. When are the times you have grown the most as a believer? What is the greatest barrier to your current spiritual growth? Are you struggling with any specific sin at this season of your life? How is God speaking to you? How is your family life going? This is a great time to grow deeper in your relationship with each other.

Take a moment to read out loud together all of the passages in this section.

FILL IN THE BLANKS

Below are the fill in the blanks for this chapter. Take a moment in the Developing Point to make sure they have these successfully filled out.

What do the parables of the mustard seed and the leaven teach us about the growth of the Kingdom?

Mustard Seed: The Kingdom of God starts small, but it grows and spreads. We should never neglect the small beginnings in our life. It is the small decisions that make the big difference.

Leaven: Jesus is reminding us that many times the Kingdom of God is producing changes in our lives that we are unaware of. As we consistently yield to God's work in our lives, He is in the process of changing us to become more like Jesus.

Who is the Holy Spirit?

The Holy Spirit is God. He is the third person of the trinity.

Why does the Holy Spirit give us spiritual gifts?

God gives us spiritual gifts to strengthen the church and impact the world.

The Kingdom of God is like a <u>MUSTARD</u> seed. It starts <u>SMALL</u>, but grows <u>LARGE</u>.

The Kingdom of God is like <u>LEAVEN</u>. We may not be able to <u>SEE</u>

everything, but that doesn't mean God is not <u>WORKING</u>.

The Holy Spirit is <u>GOD</u>.

The Holy Spirit gives us spiritual <u>GIFTS</u>.

The Holy Spirit <u>EMPOWERS</u> us to live in the Kingdom.

GOING DEEPER

The following is a list of questions from the acronym L.E.A.D that gives you a better picture into how this chapter shaped their understanding of what it means to follow Jesus.

L - LEARNING

What did you learn about the subject of growth in the Kingdom?

What did you learn about the person, role and empowering of the Holy Spirit?

What questions did you have after reading this chapter?

E - ENCOURAGED

How does understanding the subject of Kingdom growth and power encourage you as a follower of Jesus?

A - APPLYING

How does understanding the subject of Kingdom growth and the empowering of the Holy Spirit help you in your journey forward with Him?

D - DIRECT TO PRAYER

How can I pray for you this week, especially as it relates to the subject of growth and the Holy Spirit?

EXTRA QUESTIONS

Below is room for you to write down extra questions that you want to ask in your time together.

ASSIGNMENT FOR NEXT WEEK

Each week give the person you are discipling an assignment for next week. Have them write it down in the notes section of their guide.

Ask them to consider an area to serve at the church. If they are already serving, thank them for using their gifts for Kingdom purposes.

NOTES

PART 6:
COMMAND &
COMMISSION
IN THE KINGDOM

PART 6:
COMMAND &
COMMISSION

QUICK SUMMARY

The goal of this chapter is to help the person being discipled learn about the central command and commission of Jesus. They should be able to understand the following terms: loving God, loving others, loving ourselves, great commission, etc

PRAY THE KINGDOM PRAYER

Father in Heaven your Kingdom come in me and through me today. Amen!

STARTING POINT

In the very beginning take some time to share about your personal love life. If you are married, share about your marriage, if you are single, share about your hopes and dreams. Ask them to do the same. Then transition by making the connection that in this chapter we are going to look at the command of God to love.

Take a moment to read out loud together all of the passages in this section.

FILL IN THE BLANKS

Below are the fill in the blanks for this chapter. Take a moment in the Developing Point to make sure they have these successfully filled out.

What is the greatest command in the Bible?

To Love.

How do we come to the point of really loving ourselves?

We love ourself out of learning to love God. When we understand we are loved, we then can give love.

What types of people are difficult/easy for you to love?

Share your thoughts and then find out their thoughts.

What does the great commission teach us?

God has called us to go and make disciples.

What is the difference between the great command and the great commission?

They are very similar. The great command is to love God first and foremost. The great commission is to go and make disciples of all nations.

The command Jesus gave us is an UPWARD, INWARD and OUTWARD command.

It is only out of our love for GOD that we are able to love OTHERS and OURSELVES.

All of us are AMBASSADORS of Jesus Christ to those who do not know Jesus.

Discipleship is simply helping someone become a <u>FULLY DEVOTED</u> follower of Jesus Christ.

Our role is to <u>TELL</u> others about Jesus; God's role is to <u>CHANGE</u> their heart.

GOING DEEPER

The following is a list of questions from the acronym L.E.A.D that gives you a better picture into how this chapter shaped their understanding of what it means to follow Jesus.

L - LEARNING

What did you learn about the subject of love?

What did you learn about the importance of the great commission?

Find out if the person has ever been on a short term mission trip. If not encourage them to go on a trip.

What questions did you have after reading this chapter?

E - ENCOURAGED

How does understanding the subject of the great command and the great commission encourage you as a follower of Jesus?

A - APPLYING

How does understanding the subject of the great command and great commission help you in your journey forward with Him?

D - DIRECT TO PRAYER

How can I pray for you this week, especially as it relates to the subject of loving God and loving others?

EXTRA QUESTIONS

Below is room for you to write down extra questions that you want to ask in your time together.

ASSIGNMENT FOR NEXT WEEK

Each week give the person you are discipling an assignment for next week. Have them write it down in the notes section of their guide.

In preparation for the next and final week, ask them to honestly consider how they are doing at engaging in the following spiritual disciplines; rest, financial stewardship, and worship.

NOTES

PART 7:
DISCIPLINES & DISCERNMENT
IN THE KINGDOM

PART 7:
DISCIPLINES &
DISCERNMENT

QUICK SUMMARY

The goal of this chapter is to help the person being discipled learn about spiritual disciplines and discernment. They should be able to understand the following terms: sabbath, worship, stewardship, general will of God, specific will of God, etc.

PRAY THE KINGDOM PRAYER

Father in Heaven your Kingdom come in me and through me today. Amen!

STARTING POINT

In the very beginning take some time to talk about engaging in the disciplines of rest, financial stewardship, and worship. Talk about the challenges and blessings that come along with each discipline. Be open, honest, and intentional.

Take a moment to read out loud together all of the passages in this section.

FILL IN THE BLANKS

Below are the fill in the blanks for this chapter. Take a moment in the Developing Point to make sure they have these successfully filled out.

What is a spiritual discipline?

A practice that we put in place to help us center on God's purposes and agenda.

What is the spiritual discipline of rest?

Taking time on a regular basis to cease from work in order to be refueled and restored. It is an act of trust.

What is the spiritual discipline of stewardship?

The practice of managing resources in a way that honors and glorifies God.

What is the difference between a tithe and an offering?

Tithing is giving ten percent of your income to God as an aspect of worship. Offering is any giving above and beyond a tithe.

What is the spiritual discipline of worship?

The practice of honoring God, praising God and celebrating God despite circumstances or situations.

What is spiritual discernment?

The ability to understand what God is doing and how he might be leading.

What is the difference between God's general will and specific will?

General will is the general way in which God is working in the world. Specific will is the specific way in which God is working your life.

Spiritual disciplines help us focus on God's Kingdom <u>AGENDA</u>.

The word used for rest in the Bible is the word <u>SABBATH</u>.

Stewardship is managing what God has <u>ENTRUSTED</u> to us.

The opposite of worship is <u>IDOLATRY</u>.

God has a <u>GENERAL</u> will and <u>SPECIFIC</u> will for our life.

GOING DEEPER

The following is a list of questions from the acronym L.E.A.D that gives you a better picture into how this chapter shaped their understanding of what it means to follow Jesus.

L - LEARNING

What did you learn about the subject of spiritual disciplines?

What did you learn about the importance of discernment?

Find out if they are struggling to discover God's specific will in an area.

What questions did you have after reading this chapter?

E - ENCOURAGED

How does understanding the subject of spiritual disciplines and discernment encourage you as a follower of Jesus?

A - APPLYING

How does understanding the subject of spiritual disciplines and discernment help you in your journey forward with Him?

D - DIRECT TO PRAYER

How can I pray for you this week, especially as it relates to the subject of spiritual disciplines and discernment?

EXTRA QUESTION

Below is room for you to write down extra questions that you want to ask in your time together.

CELEBRATING THE END

As you finish your time with the person you have been discipling, thank them, pray for them and consider setting up a separate time just to eat dinner and celebrate the time that you spent with each other.

NOTES

Made in the USA
San Bernardino, CA
08 May 2016